THE GRAPHIC ARTIST'S GUIDE TO
MARKETING AND
SELF-PROMOTION

Sally Prince Davis

NORTH LIGHT BOOKS Cincinnati, Ohio

Published by North Light Books, an imprint of F&W Publications, Inc., 1507 Dana Ave., Cincinnati, Ohio 45207.

Manufactured in U.S.A.

Library of Congress Cataloging-in-Publication Data

Davis, Sally Prince, 1942-
    The graphic artist's guide to marketing and self-promotion.

    Bibliography: p.
    Includes index.
    1. Graphic arts—Marketing. 2. Sales promotion. I. Title.
NC1001.6.D38   1987   741.6'068'8   87-7868
ISBN 0-89134-192-7

Editor: Diana Martin
Designer: Carol Buchanan

To Garry, Bryse, and Zach

CONTENTS

CHAPTER 1

THE CHALLENGE OF FREE-LANCING 1

Free-lance Opportunities 2
Dealing with Rejection—and Success 6
Working from Your Own Studio 11
Setting Up for Business 13

CHAPTER 2

MARKETING AND SELF-PROMOTION: THE ESSENTIALS 19

Nuts and Bolts Terminology 19
Marketing: What Is It, and How Do You Do It? 20
Identifying Your Product's Strengths and Weaknesses 22
Finding the Right Market for Your Product 24
Self-Promotion: The Art of Blowing Your Own Horn 26

CHAPTER 3

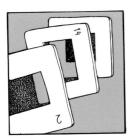

TOOLS OF THE TRADE 37

Art Samples 37
Design Samples 47
Photographing Your Artwork 48
Developing Your Portfolio 51
Printed Marketing Tools 51
Writing Marketing Copy That Sells 77

CHAPTER 4
PULLING IT ALL TOGETHER 83

Market Research: How to Find Clients 83
Developing Your Marketing Tools 88

CHAPTER 5
THE BUSINESS OF MARKETING 95

Organizing and Following a Marketing Plan 95
Local Self-Promotion 99
Advertising in Creative Services Books 101
Approaching the Client 102
Determining and Negotiating a Price 106
Updating Your Marketing Strategy 112
The Changing Graphic Art Scene 114

RESOURCES 116

Directories 116
Periodicals 116
Creative Services Books 118
Organizations 118

INDEX 119

ACKNOWLEDGMENTS

A book of this type is never accomplished alone and I gratefully acknowledge the willingness of all of the graphic artists and art directors to share their insight and promotional pieces. I also thank editors Diana Martin and Christine Cotting and art director Carol Buchanan for their expert and always cheerful advice and assistance.

ABOUT THE AUTHOR

Sally Prince Davis, a former editor of the annual directory *Artist's Market,* is now a free-lance writer and art marketing consultant. She also writes the monthly "Strictly Business" column for *The Artist's Magazine* and is a popular speaker on the business side of art at art workshops, conferences, and seminars around the country.

INTRODUCTION

Today's free-lance graphic artist competes in two worlds: creative and business. Although graphic artists routinely arm themselves creatively through art classes and practice, they seldom acquire the business know-how and marketing savvy needed to find the art directors interested in their type of work and to land the assignments that are artistically and monetarily fulfilling. Consequently, art school graduates and self-taught graphic artists alike are forced to learn the business side of their art the hard way, through mistakes and perseverance, or to give up entirely on their dream of free-lancing, of being their own boss, because they can't make enough money to live solely from their talent.

No longer. I wrote this book to fill that void in business knowledge—to help you, as a graphic artist, reduce your mistakes, increase your persistence, and make a free-lance career a reality. Here are the marketing and self-promotion basics that will allow you to take your careers into your own hands. Adapt these basics to your own situation and goals, whether graphic art is a full-time or part-time career or simply an avocation through which you earn spare money and the satisfaction of seeing your work published.

This book focuses only on marketing and self-promotion in order to cover comprehensively these important building blocks of your business knowledge. It provides a discussion of the purposes of marketing and self-promotion, how to determine who and where the clients are for your type(s) of work, the tools to develop to reach these clients, and exactly how to contact them. This book is geared to you graphic artists who are beginning to market your work, but who are not necessarily new artists, and you experienced artists seeking new ways to increase your business. Thus, it is written with a presumption of knowledge on your part regarding graphic art materials, skills, and techniques.

During my four years as editor of *Artist's Market,* I heard repeatedly the frustration of talented artists whose work, for no apparent reason, wouldn't sell and, conversely the complaints of art directors about inappropriate or insufficient contact from artists. I am pleased to have the opportunity to use the knowledge I gained through this editorial "liaison" role and through personal experience to help bridge the marketing and communications gap that exists between graphic artist and art director. Your only obligation is to use this information as a strong foundation upon which to build your art career. Use it to understand the unknowns and to approach marketing and self-promotion with the confidence your artwork deserves.

—Sally Prince Davis

CHAPTER 1
THE CHALLENGE OF FREE-LANCING

Graphic art shapes the artistic tastes of the average person—it's the artwork that surrounds us daily. The billboards we read on our way to work, the hangtags on the clothes we buy, the ads and illustrations in the magazines in our homes—these are the works of art that we relate to, that attract our attention and compel us to an emotional reaction, conscious or not, every day.

Graphic art is, by definition, simply illustration and design, but its impact is widespread. Its communication value is respected and utilized by all segments of the for-profit and not-for-profit communities. It's the corporate logo that visually transmits the company "image" at a glance; the book cover that conveys a feeling or plot through one illustration; the package design that identifies a product before the name is read; the editorial illustration that enhances the written word; the record-album cover that captures the essence of the recording star as well as the music; the brochure that defines a performing-arts group.

Graphic artists and designers are visual communicators who are willing to confine their creativity to serving the specific purpose of an assignment. While following public demand, these artists and designers also set their own trends, expanding the public's imagination through visual encounters. To belong to this remarkable group of people is to accept artistic challenge, business ingenuity, and public-relations resourcefulness as parts of life.

For the free-lance graphic artist or designer, artistic knowledge, skill, talent, and style have been so refined that together they form a marketable product: work that meets the needs of clients. Some free-lancers' belief in their own ability is reinforced by years of experience as an in-house employee in a graphic arts field, perhaps as a staff illustrator for a greeting card company, designer with an art or design studio, or an ad agency art director. Others have just graduated from art school and don't want a position as a permanent employee—they want to try it on their own first. For yet others, graphic art is an avocation, a serious pastime regularly scheduled but not relied upon for a substantial portion of income.

Three desires are normally expressed through the decision to free-lance:

- To have the world perceive you as a creative person.
- To make money through your art and design.
- To have the freedom to choose when, where, and how you work.

The big questions concern how you make these desires reality:

- How do you let potential art buyers know about your creativity and talent and in turn reach the public with your artistic vision?
- How do you organize and operate a business?
- How do you get profitable assignments?

The answers lie in marketing your work, promoting yourself as a graphic artist, and learning the business side of art.

A successful free-lancer must be a business person, art director, and public-relations manager while remaining a graphic artist. Free-lancing requires the self-discipline of a small-business owner to keep records, understand business legalities, and regulate finances; the ability of an art director to identify one's role within a creative project and maintain a studio; the hustle and communications ability of a public-relations manager to promote oneself to potential clients.

The benefits of free-lancing include the freedom to set one's own work hours, be one's own boss, and apply a medley of abilities to one's own personal and business goals.

FREE-LANCE OPPORTUNITIES

The range of markets available to free-lance graphic artists is nearly limitless—all you have to do is look around you at the magazines, books, advertisements, television commercials, calendars, business correspondence, packages, and signs to know that graphic art is in demand.

The producers of these products, and more, are all graphic art markets, but they differ in the number of free-lance art they use and how they work with graphic artists. Some market fields are more accessible to free-lance artists because they are willing to work with graphic artists through the mail or in person and they use large amounts of artwork. Others are open to working both ways, but realistically don't offer the sales possibilities as do the high-volume markets. And yet others are market fields where art directors prefer to work with artists who live close by so they can sit in on client meetings, be available at a moment's notice and turn work around quickly, often overnight. In these fields, some firms will work with artists through the mail,

but the occurrence is low and usually reserved for well-known artists whose particular style has been sought out.

Where you live greatly affects the market areas you'll approach. Artists in large urban centers can consider a variety of market areas because they have the option of taking advantage of working both in person and by mail. Artists living in small towns, however, might find their local market areas, their in-person contacts, very limited and will have to do most of their assignments, and therefore their marketing, via the mail.

The following general descriptions of market areas for you to consider are broken down according to their accessibility to artists and volume of art used. The first group is that in which firms generally are willing to work by mail and their volume of art purchases makes them most open to contact by free-lance artists; this doesn't prohibit a graphic artist from contacting these types of firms in person, however. The second group will also work with artists by mail, but not to the extent as the first, and the amount of work they buy is somewhat less. The third group, generally speaking, prefers to work with local artists and are the least open to working by mail. On the whole, the amount of free-lance work they buy is medium to high.

Markets to Contact by Mail: High Volume Sales

The marketing areas that fall into this category are magazines, greeting card publishers, book publishers, clip art firms, and art publishers and distributors.

Magazines

Periodical publications offer opportunities for editorial and cover illustrations, cartoons, and design. Both beginners and established pros are needed by magazines of various types, sizes, and circulations. Specialized skills and subjects, such as medical, scientific, and technical illustration, have an outlet in journals and periodicals.

The larger the circulation or reputation of the publication, the greater the pay *and* the competition. Smaller or lesser-known publications act as launching pads for beginners: they are willing to overlook an artist's lack of experience in exchange for lower fees or payment in complimentary copies.

Greeting Card Publishers

Some publishers only consider illustrations for card ideas that have been developed in-house; others are willing to review entire card concepts—including design, illustration and text—created and submitted by free-lancers. Paper-product firms—those that produce napkins, stationery, invitations, note cards—are usually considered in the same context as greeting card publishers, since their art needs and consumer audience are similar. Work for such firms offers the possibility of added income from product licensing of characters originally developed through a line of cards.

Book Publishers

These firms use graphic artists for book design, text illustration, and jacket or cover illustration. New free-lancers can often break into this market first through the small publisher, but the larger publishers are not entirely out of reach. Such collateral materials as posters, displays, and promotional materials offer additional opportunities with these buyers.

Most publishing art directors look for graphic artists who can capture and transmit the overall feeling of a book through its design and enhance written words with illustration.

Clip Art Firms

Clip art firms' sole purpose is to supply camera-ready illustrations, cartoons, spot drawings and decorative art to other individuals and businesses for a fee. Their clients pay for this service and use the art in their ads, newsletters, letterheads—indeed, any way they want to. Clip art firms usually supply the art in varying sizes on sheets or in booklets which the client simply cuts apart. Black-and-white line, easily reproduced artwork usually sells best to these firms, which frequently pay a flat fee per illustration.

Art Publishers and Distributors

Companies that publish and/or distribute those prints and posters that the public has fallen in love with are called art publishers and distributors. A publisher pays you for the right to reproduce your work as a print, sometimes a flat fee, sometimes a royalty, and usually handles the sale and distribution. Art distributors only distribute prints that you've already reproduced (usually at your own expense); artists usually receive a royalty on each print sold or sell the prints to the distributor outright at a wholesale price. Original artwork offered to these firms should possess clarity of line, clear color and subject matter that appeals to the masses since these modestly priced works are often thought of as decorative accessories.

Markets to Contact by Mail or In Person: Medium Volume Sales

Everything being relative, of course,

these marketing areas generally don't use or buy as much artwork as those above, but certainly offer sound sales opportunities.

Newspaper and Newsletter Publishers

These publications encompass a great deal of diversity—inhouse newsletters, national and regional newspapers, tabloids, weeklies, and dailies, to name only a few. Most don't use color, so black-and-white illustrations do best here. Cartoons and editorial illustrations are their primary needs, but a paper nearby might also require ad illustration and design work. Try contacting your local newspaper first, then branch out to publishers across the country. A newsletter can have a national subscription or be the house organ for a specific company. Contact area firms to determine their newsletter production procedure and let them know your interest in supplying artwork.

Associations

All associations are interested in public exposure and many achieve it through posters, mailings, catalogs, newsletters and magazines, all of which utilize art. Each association also possesses a specific interest and "image," so artists who specialize in a particular type of art might research associations that share the same interest. Budgets are sometimes tight, so many associations are seeking artists who can produce captivating, yet low cost, art and design. But success here can lead to landing the assignment for a high-budget, complex campaign when it comes along.

Institutions

Like associations, institutions such as hospitals, colleges and universities, seek to get their message to the public and often rely on artwork to prompt people to pick up their brochures or read their catalogs. Start with the institutions nearest you and contact the public relations or communications director to see how you might be utilized on a free-lance basis. If you find that you excel in a specific area, such as medical illustration, then consider contacting hospitals nationwide for additional assignments.

Performing Arts Groups

The graphic artist providing art and design to these groups often faces the challenge of communicating to the public the group's "image" in conjunction with a particular performance, of supplying artwork whose elements can be separated to carry a theme through different printed pieces, and of doing this for a very reasonable price especially if the group is nonprofit. But if you thrive on artwork that focuses on music, dance, theatre and opera then these groups can provide a good marketing field for you to investigate.

Record Companies

These firms use graphic artists not only for album covers, but also many of the peripheral items, such as posters, point-of-purchase displays, mobiles and promotional materials. Each record company specializes in a particular type of music and wants art that communicates its specialty to the consumer. Album covers must be eye-catching while visually integrating the artistic image of the recording artist with the music inside.

Syndicates

Syndicates act as middlemen between artist and publications; if a syndicate accepts the work of an artist, it then promotes and sells it to publications nationally and, in some cases, worldwide. Cartoons, single panel and strip, are the artwork usually thought of in conjunction with syndicates, but some accept spot drawings and illustrations to go with columns, such as cooking, advice and astrology columns. If you're developing a cartoon strip for consideration by a syndicate, study those that are already in newspapers and have at least several weeks' worth ready before submission.

Markets to Contact In Person: Medium to High Volume Sales

The four categories of marketing fields here are the ones that generally prefer local artists for quick accessibility, but mail contact is not out of the question. As general fields, these firms buy and use large amounts of art, but the amount of sales generated for an individual artist depends on the size of the firm contacted.

Advertising Agencies

We're all familiar with the numerous print ads that appear in our magazines and newspapers, and it's the job of ad agencies to create them. These firms frequently work on short deadlines and under pressure, and, depending on the size of the agency, can need artwork for one ad or an entire, year-long campaign. Many agencies specialize in particular types of clients and will search for artists whose work meets that specialization. Since agencies must please their own clients, artists who are available to sit in on client meetings can have the advantage of hearing firsthand what the client is expecting. Some agencies that handle television commercials might also expect their artists to have skill in creating storyboards, computer graphics or animation.

Public Relations Firms

Conveying a message to the public is the chief priority of these firms. Depending on the size of the firm, it might assume responsibility for revitalizing the public image of a major corporation from logo to advertisements or develop a single brochure for a small business. Art needs in these firms vary because they are keyed to supplying whatever their clients need. These firms don't have quite the pressure that ad agencies do, but a quick-turnaround job can mean needing an artist *now*. Artists who enjoy corporate art, logos and designing literature such as brochures should consider PR firms as a marketing field.

Art/Design Studios

These studios are, in a sense, doing exactly what you're doing—meeting the art and design needs of their clients. Some studios are one-person operations; when the workload becomes too much, that person turns to a free-lancer to help out. Others are large operations capable of supplying everything to a client—art, design, photography, and printing. These studios use free-lancers regularly to do single illustrations or to handle entire projects. Many studios specialize in a particular type of client, but many do not—they'll handle anything that comes along. If you like variety, check out the local art/design studios since they frequently like artists nearby for quick assignments. If your work is outstanding or unusual, try contacting these studios by mail; they sometimes will work by mail on projects that have a long lead time.

Businesses

This general term, businesses, means everything from the local supermarket to the multi-million dollar corporation; indeed, any service, retail or merchandising firm. Frequently these companies have a need for graphic art and don't know where to turn to get it. They might need a quick advertisement, an annual report, an in-house newsletter, an employee brochure, or a new logo. Having your name and talent on file, especially if you possess skills such as paste-up and layout, can mean getting the full assignment instead of it being turned over to an art studio, ad agency or PR firm. Be sure all of your local businesses know that you can fill their art needs if you like this type of variety in your assignments.

DEALING WITH REJECTION—AND SUCCESS

One of the hazards of free-lancing is that you fall on your face alone; one of the pleasures is that you succeed alone. There's no one else to blame when something goes wrong, but there's no one else deserving the praise when everything is perfect.

Everyone, no matter how famous, has had to deal with rejection, that thudding "No, thank you" to your talent and skill. It's simply a part of the business, an aspect to which you eventually become accustomed. But it's still hard to deal with and—especially if there are several rejections in a row—it can be depressing.

HANDS-ON EXPERIENCE

Patie Kay, a Los Angeles free-lance graphic artist who opened her own business in 1976, was agency-trained and learned many graphic-arts skills through hands-on experience.

"I started out working on a small throw-away newspaper for which I sold display advertising. I would approach a client and say, "You'll get this size ad for this much money. What do you want in it?" They'd tell me what they wanted in it and ask me what it would look like. So I started sketching the ideas for an ad in the little squares that were going to represent what they were going to get in the paper. These sketches were turned over to the typesetter and printer. One day I got a call from him and he said, 'I love your layouts.' My response was, 'Great. What's a layout?' "

From this dubious beginning, Kay went on to work at another newspaper, where she learned about typography from typesetting to type specing, and

from there to an ad agency where "the art director was very kind. He took me under his wing and said, 'If you want to learn, I'll teach you,' and that's how I got my education. I was there for five years and in the beginning worked some horrendous hours with incredible deadlines, but eventually was responsible for releasing pieces running in the millions of copies."

Because of her background, today Kay is able to offer her clients all art services except printing. "I'll do anything—design, layout, illustration, photo retouching, color-cutting, paste-up. One of the reasons I'm successful is that I have a broad range of talent and enough education to get the job done."

Most of Kay's clients are individual companies that come to her with a specific need, such as a brochure or an annual stockholder's report, and her client list has expanded so much that she turns away jobs.

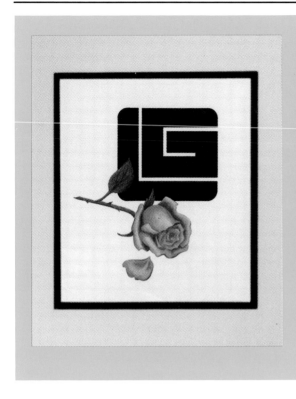

Indicative of the type and treatment of original artwork Patie Kay of Los Angeles includes in her portfolio is this matted sample of a logo design. She always uses double mats, with the outer mat a neutral color and the inner one a color complimentary to the work. Between the mats and art is a sheet of clear plastic to minimize damage from spills. She changes mats after 15-20 handlings due to smudging and bent corners.

There are several hard facts of business life that must become a part of your reality.

Hard Fact of Life Number 1

Your creativity is a business product. No matter how much of yourself is in your illustration, no matter how terrific you think a design is, if it isn't marketable, it's going to be rejected. You must view your artwork as a product and distance yourself from it as much as possible in order to evaluate it objectively and determine its suitability to a particular art buyer.

Hard Fact of Life Number 2

Your artwork is not going to please all people all of the time—and it shouldn't. For those times when it hasn't pleased (especially the times when an art director reviews your portfolio and suggests you give up art), fall back on your personal inner strength. The importance of a firm faith in yourself, your talent, and your work can't be overestimated. Balance this inner faith with rational thought—identify critical points in the negative response and weigh their validity. Certainly negativity hurts; feel the hurt, but move beyond it. Learn from constructive advice, affirm your faith in yourself, and plan for the next opportunity to market your work.

Hard Fact of Life Number 3

There will probably not be *one* sale that is going to "make it" for you. You will think that if you can just sell to this or that client you'll be on easy street. It's unlikely; rather, your career will be a series of sales, each adding to your reputation and pocketbook, but in a continuum, not a windfall. After one job is over, be looking toward the next.

If rejection does get a stranglehold on you, what can you do to break its grip?

First, keep it in perspective. Remember that rejection is only one person's opinion of your work, and that person is viewing it with individual preferences and art needs in mind. Luck and timing play nearly as important a role in this business as talent does. Your work was in the wrong place at the wrong time, and you have to move on.

Second, cultivate a support system—other artists, family, or friends to whom you can turn for empathy and/or advice. Select people to whom you can pour out your angry feelings and perhaps slightly irrational opinions of the person who rejected your work, knowing that your words will never go any further. A person who can reinforce the positive aspects of you and your talent is a boon. Such friends may be hard to find. If you're new to an area, so that time and circumstance haven't allowed enough history to pass between you and another person to build a trusting relationship, you may be forced to become your own self-esteem booster.

Releasing anger is important and point three, next, addresses that issue. But to complement the release, invent a ritual for yourself that makes you feel good and worthwhile. Once the anger and stress are exhausted, pamper yourself with a mood lifter. It's different for each of us: reading quietly for an hour, shopping, cooking, working with your hands in a non-art-related project, daydreaming, listening to music. Whatever your self-satisfying endeavors are, call on them to rejuvenate the spirit if your work is rejected.

Third, realize that rejection makes you feel rebuffed and unappreciated and generates anger. Suppressed anger can lead to dejection, serious depression, a drop in self-confidence, and artist's block. *Don't keep anger inside*—vent it to that trusted friend mentioned earlier, if possible. If not, remember that anger is energy waiting for release, so get rid of it by performing any exercise that dissipates it without hurting others or jeopardizing your good reputation. You might punch a pillow, go jogging, do aerobics, walk, swim, run in place, pursue a hobby that demands physical exertion—but find some activity that burns up negative energy and leaves your spirit balanced and ready for positive input.

Fourth, lessen the possibility for future rejections. Research markets thoroughly, approach outlets most appropriate for your work, and evaluate your business materials. Do your printed promotional pieces need updating? Are they communicating your talent and experience as well as they can? Is it time to examine your career to see if you've subtly changed direction and need now to investigate new market areas?

This might also be the time to examine how you *really feel* about being a graphic artist. Not everyone can accept the day-in, day-out reconstruction of creative vision by clients. Some graphic artists still operate with the unconscious belief that somehow graphic art is "less" than fine art because it's created for a commercial purpose. Some of you may even believe that to receive payment for your work is "selling out" and dishonorable: "real" artists pursue examination of and excellence in their artform alone, never to be sold, the rest of the world be hanged. Such feelings and beliefs can sabotage your career by unconsciously setting you up for rejection because you feel you are pursuing a less-than-worthwhile life's work.

Well, pardon my bluntness but, hogwash to all these beliefs. Yes, I know these opinions are out there and that the feelings exist; I'm not denying that. But they're so outdated, such holdovers from times that have long since passed that to keep playing those same scripts over and over is unnecessary. Yes, it is difficult to have someone, perhaps with much less talent than you (or no talent at all), tell you why they don't like the illustration you did and the changes that need to be made to keep the client happy. But graphic artists aren't singled out here—no creative endeavor is without critics and change. That's why editors revise the words of writers (this one included), directors tell actors and actresses how to perform, musicians follow a conductor. All of us artists bring as much of our special vision as we can into our works, listen to the input of knowledgeable others, and then work hand-in-hand to create the best result possible. A graphic artist who meets the needs of a client is allowing a creative interpretation of this assignment to be seen and appreciated by the public; the graphic artist who sticks to the old "my way or else" is more likely to have work turned down, never to be seen at all.

Compared with the previous century, society's attitudes have shifted, yet retained an influence of the past. In the 1800s, graphic art was considered the most honorable and secure of professions: graphic artists were frequently used to advertise products because they were people to be looked up to, the communicators of the nation's progress. Lithography and wood engraving had brought pictures to books, magazines, and newspapers; drawings of machinery and buildings were needed to move forward the spreading industrialization. There was a hunger to *see* what was going on, not simply read about it. Thus to be a graphic artist was a high goal: parents encouraged children, workshops were offered, art schools sprang up to foster it. The wealthy—those who didn't have to work for a living—pursued fine or decorative art, usually but not always as a pastime. This division of the classes is the basis for attitudes still held by some today—that to create art for a commercial purpose and sell it means you must work for a living and therefore are not among the favored few pursuing art for art's sake (who, of course, were "better" because they were wealthy). I think we'd all agree that these nineteenth-century attitudes simply don't apply to today's world—so why keep laboring under them? Don't sabotage yourself with such silly, outmoded beliefs.

Success, strange though it seems, also has pitfalls. For the sake of simplicity, success is here defined in monetary terms.

When high-paying jobs begin to come your way, the sudden influx of money can create pressures you didn't have when you were a relative unknown. Money management is crucial; the understandable tendency is to blow the money on luxuries you couldn't afford before. Don't. Your income will plateau and possibly even drop slightly, but payments on those luxury items remain the same. By saving or investing at least part of the money, you'll ensure a future with fewer money worries. Be kind to yourself—buy one "toy," but keep your lifestyle basically the same until you're certain the big jobs are here to stay.

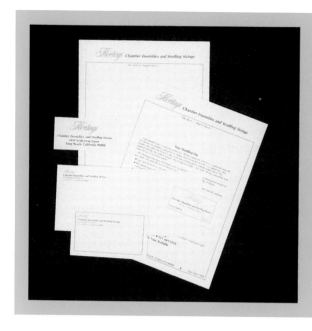

Tearsheets of work completed for clients are also a part of Kay's portfolio. She puts them in individual envelopes and carries them in the pockets of her portfolio for quick access in a review. Because she believes art buyers like to handle the actual materials she always requests ten copies of every assignment so she can change tearsheets when they become soiled.

As they command higher and higher prices for their art and design, some artists begin to feel the pressure of trying to live up to their reputations. Each assignment is expected to be "worthy" of the high fees, yet clients want the same "look" so that it has that unmistakably recognizable mark. Artists in this position find themselves trapped between trying to top their last assignment and wanting—needing—to grow creatively. Some react by overindulging in drugs or alcohol or by suffering artist's block.

It goes without saying that neither drugs nor alcohol is the answer. In the long and short run they dull your creative edge and rob you of valuable artistic time. Temporary artist's block can be overcome by relaxing with a pen or pencil in your hand, by leaving the project and returning to it at a later time, or by trying to determine the reason for the block—fear of failure, fatigue, worry over an extraneous problem. If the artist's block persists until it's endangering your ca-

reer, however, don't be afraid to seek professional counseling.

Some psychologists, psychiatrists, and other psychotherapists specialize in treating creative people and understand their pressures and blocks, but such specialists aren't available in every city or town. Nonspecialized, trained professionals in these fields can help you to understand the underlying causes of your block; the block is a symptom, not the disease. So even if you can't find one who specializes in creative people, seek out a professional with whom you feel comfortable, who understands what you're experiencing, and who listens to you. I know these are general statements, but it's extremely difficult to be more specific when needs are so individual.

To find the right professional sometimes means searching and asking questions. If you have artist friends or an art association to which you can turn for first-hand-experience referrals, do so. Listen to what these people did and didn't like about the professional and judge for yourself if this is someone you'd like to approach for counseling. You can also look in the Yellow Pages under various headings—Mental Health Services, Psychologists, Psychiatrists (often under Physicians & Surgeons), Psychotherapists, Counselors—to find the names of professionals and clinics that might meet your needs. Some communities offer a referral service to provide the names of several professionals who might help your situation. This type of service is usually listed under Mental Health Services in the Yellow Pages or by name in the white pages. Many crisis lines, mental health hospitals, and national health organizations (if branches are in your city) will also offer referral service. When selecting the professional to help you through your block, remember—ask questions about his or her training and qualifications; you have the right to be comfortable and knowledgeable in this relationship.

Most of all, to avoid the pitfalls and to enjoy your success to the fullest, think of it as a single point in a continuing line. Grow as an artist, even if you lose some clients because your art has taken on a new look and they still want the identifiable old look. You know yourself best as a creative person; if success and high finances have you feeling stagnant and stale, be confident and financially secure enough to stretch and reach out in a new artistic direction.

WORKING FROM YOUR OWN STUDIO

It sounds luxurious to work in casual clothes, with no time clock to punch and no harrowing drive to the studio. And it is.

But hand-in-hand with these plusses for the independent artist go tremendous needs for self-discipline, a regular number of work hours, an ability to convince others that you're running a business, and a self-imposed professional attitude.

Problems encountered with an independent studio are:

■ *Isolation.* There's no one around to stimulate creativity, to handle building paperwork, or to help untangle business problems. You're entirely on your own. You must learn to criticize and praise your own endeavors, to routinely take care of office duties, and to know when to call in outside professionals—accountants, tax specialists, attorneys—to resolve business situations that aren't routine.

■ *Temptation.* Whether it's the refrigerator or the television set, a golf game or dirty dishes, temptation rears its head and tries to keep you from working. Entire workdays can disappear unless you establish a regular number of work hours and stick to them. Taking "a minute" to fold the laundry or to finish that magazine article can actually steal an hour away from your business day. You don't submit to these temptations if there is a boss in someone else's company to answer to—why is it legitimate to do it to *your* "company"?

■ *Family and friends.* These well-meaning people interrupt at will because they know you're "available"; somehow your "freedom" translates into not being busy or not *really* working. You find yourself responsible for solving problems or running errands during your workday. Learn to say no or schedule demands around your work hours. Daycare or babysitting arrangements should be made for children if their care is cutting significantly into your work hours.

Again I'm going to stress the establishment of regular work hours, complete with scheduled coffee and meal breaks. You are now a self-employed business person and have to conduct yourself as such. As you cultivate this business attitude with friends and family, there will be fewer interruptions because they know you are serious about your work. In addition, you'll reinforce the attitude within your own mind. When you walk into the studio/office area, you'll be "at work," and other aspects of your life will fade while you get down to the serious business of pursuing your art career.

■ *Clients' attitudes.* Some clients respect artists less if they discover they're meeting in a home studio. Some even go so far as to expect lower fees because the artist doesn't have a "real" place of business. Counteract this response with *your* professional attitude, that of a business person whose art knowledge and skill are ready to meet the needs of the client. Demonstrate that you are ready and able to conduct business regardless of the setting.

■ *The jeans dream.* At your own studio there's a temptation to be casual in dress and personal hygiene; be aware that your appearance communicates a message to the client—as do your attitude and surroundings. If you're hosting a client meeting, clean the meeting space, change into clothes you would wear at the client's office, have all necessary materials at your fingertips, and be ready when he or she arrives. You're demonstrating, as you should, that you take yourself and your art career seriously.

■ *Makeshift environment.* Business is business and home is home—except when the two are mingled. Work-ing from home means you're transforming living space into work space. At best you're disrupting only your own life; at worst, you're asking other family members to accommodate themselves to smaller living quarters.

Ideally, if you live in a single-family home with other family members, your studio/office is a building separate from the main part of the house. A converted garage or outbuilding works well for this purpose; a basement with a separate entrance also suffices, if not as a studio, at least as a space for client conferences. If this isn't possible, at least house your business activities in a separate room, such as a converted extra bedroom, den, or study. Provide comfortable seating within this area for client meetings, a door that can be closed, and soundproofing. Inform family members that *no* interruptions are allowed while you're meeting with a client.

If you live alone (or nearly so) in a small apartment or loft, especially one where a space totally separate from living areas isn't possible, build or buy inexpensive screens to set up or hang divider curtains from the ceiling. If you can't use either of these suggestions, give serious thought to what you *can* do to cut yourself off visually from the rest of the living areas. You deserve a quiet, private place to work, free from the distractions of the rest of your life regardless of whether or not a client ever steps foot in the door.

■ *Privacy.* If you have your home phone number on business cards or meet clients in your home, expect to lose some privacy and security. A separate business telephone alleviates the disruption of your personal phone; a phone answering machine can be connected if you don't like to be disturbed while you're working. Speaker devices that allow you to monitor the calls as they come in mean you can answer urgent calls immediately. Remaining firm about stating very specific hours during which you will meet with clients in your home helps to diminish the number who feel they can show up any time because "you work at home." If you don't want to meet clients in your home, you can always suggest meeting in their offices or at a restaurant, hotel lobby, or conference room, if appropriate to the meeting's purpose. A post office box allows mail deliveries without disclosure of your home address.

SETTING UP FOR BUSINESS

Your studio is equipped for creating art, but is it prepared to conduct an art business? Marketing, self-promotion, and record keeping—the business of art—must become as much a part of you as illustration and design if your art business is to be organized and successful.

To promote a business environment and give yourself adequate space for business activities, your studio should contain a desk (or large flat table), file cabinet, bookcase, storage rack or area, and a good desk lamp. If your actual studio space isn't large enough to accommodate office furniture, set up an area nearby that is yours for business when you need it. These pieces can frequently be placed in living areas without disruption if space is at a premium.

Two other pieces of business machinery have become more important as the age of technology incorporates itself into our daily lives: the computer and the copier. This equipment has both art and business applications. For a look at one artist's use of

both for marketing and business management, see the sidebar on pages 14 and 15.

Besides your office furnishings and equipment, another important aspect to a functioning business is solid, consistent record keeping. It's time consuming, but vital to your personal knowledge of how you're doing financially and to the Internal Revenue Service when taxes fall due (which, depending on your income and filing method, may be every three months or even more frequently). Many of your expenses to run your art business qualify as tax deductions, and you don't want to miss out on rightfully claiming them.

Record keeping doesn't have to be extremely complicated, especially while business transactions are few. A hardcover columnar record book suffices; you can find one at a discount, office supply, or stationery store. You can also purchase columnar record books with pull-out pages and three-ring holes, ideal for inserting in a notebook cover as needed. Mark one section for *Income* and another for *Expenses;* keep all receipts from every purchase made for the art business. An accordion file or folders labeled by month make this process easy.

If your transactions are sufficient to warrant a more detailed accounting of income and expenses, pages in the record book can be labeled to coincide with the information the IRS requires on its business tax form, Schedule C of Form 1040, Profit or (Loss) from Business or Profession. Filling out this form is less complicated if you've kept track of your expenses. Record them under such headings as Dues and Publications, Office/Studio Expenses, Office/Studio Supplies, Utilities and Telephone, Le-

THE COMPUTER-PHOTOCOPIER ONE-TWO

Richard Orlin, a fulltime cartoonist and Charles M. Schulz Award winner who recently moved from the Bronx, New York, to Alexandria, Virginia, has found that using a personal home computer and photocopier has made some aspects of conducting business cheaper and faster.

When marketing panel gag cartoons to magazines, Orlin mails out a cover letter, resume, promotional card, business card, and, in most instances, one or two cartoon samples appropriate to the publication. All of these marketing materials are produced through his personal computer and photocopier.

"I keep a mailing list of about 225 names of cartoon outlets on my computer. I use *Writer's Digest, Artist's Market,* and lists and newsletters available through cartoonists' organizations to identify potential markets. When I get some new names, I do a mailing and then add these names to the master list on my computer.

"My cover letter and resume are also on my computer. For each mailing, all I have to do is fill in the appropriate name and address on the letter and print it and the resume out on my printer. If I should make a typing mistake, I can correct it on the screen *before* it's printed, making this whole process easier than if I were using a typewriter. The cover letter and resume are on half-sheets of paper, 5½ by 8½-inches, so they're the same size as my promo card and all fit neatly into a small, 6½ by 9½-inch, envelope.

"I use a home photocopier to reproduce my promo card and business card on card stock. The personal copier was the best business investment I ever made. I use it not only for the cards, but also to make copies of my cartoon samples and multiple copies of invoices and reply cards that have been originally printed out via the computer. The computer's printer is dot matrix but is near letter quality. Photocopying helps to close the spaces between the dots, giving an even closer appearance to printing.

"When I do a promotional card, I have to draw the cartoons to the size they'll be on the card, since the copier doesn't reduce or enlarge. If I were buying a photocopier today, I'd definitely buy one that has these capabilities. Since I can't do typesetting, the written information for the card is produced on the computer, using a program that gives me a choice of approximately thirty different type styles. I paste up the cartoons and the written text and then photocopy as many cards as I need at the time.

"I save a lot of money in printing costs this way because I can change my materials when I want to. I market both panel gag cartoons and humorous illustrations, so I need promo cards, cover letters, and art samples that are different in each marketing effort. I also do very small mailings and especially slant my cartoons to the market I'm sending to; for example, I mail cartoons with legal themes to law magazines.

"I'd spend forty dollars to have 2,000 promo cards offset printed in black and white. I've figured it costs me a little under four cents a sheet to do my own copying, so it is slightly more costly than offset printing. But there's no waste because I can do the type of card I

RICHARD ORLIN, 6101 Edsall Rd #1704, Alexandria, VA 22304 (703)370-5108
Clients: Mobil Oil Corp, Good Housekeeping, Better Homes & Gardens, National Lampoon, American Medical Assoc., TV Guide, National Enquirer
Awards: Carles Schulz Award, Scripps Howard Foundation

RICHARD ORLIN
Clients: Mobil Oil Corp., Good Housekeeping, Better Homes & Gardens, National Lampoon, American Medical Assoc., TV Guide, National Enquirer

Reproducing promotional cards on his photocopier lets Richard Orlin customize them to his market areas.

want when I want it and only the specific number I need. If I had 2,000 of them, I'd end up using them as scrap paper. Also I don't have to drive to the printer or copy shop.

"I paid around $800 for my copier when I bought it about three years ago and they've gone down in price since. Cartridges (the replaceable portion of the machine that holds the toner or "ink") cost fifty to seventy-five dollars each, depending on where and how many you buy. How long you can use each cartridge depends on how much you use the machine, of course, but each one is good for about 1,500 to 2,000 copies of a standard letter. I save money by buying paper in bulk.

"My investment in my computer and printer was about $600 and the software cost $13 for SpeedScript (order through *Compute!* magazine) and $40 for Fontmaster II. I've had absolutely no maintenance costs whatsoever for the photocopier. I think the money was definitely well spent and, for the artist who works in black and white, even if he has to take out a loan for the initial investment, it's worth it in the long run."

gal and Professional Services, Travel and Entertainment, Car and Truck Expenses (which might include mileage if you select that method of accounting). This list is not comprehensive; it suggests deductions free-lancers commonly encounter in running their businesses. More detailed accounting takes place if you're deducting your studio as a home office, have bad debts (uncollected fees for work you submitted), and so on. If such further deductions apply to you, contact an accountant for advice. Many accountants will set up books for you for a fee.

Remember, too, that running your own business means keeping up on trends in your field. To do this, subscribe to and read graphic arts magazines such as *Communication Arts, Print, Step-by-Step Graphics* and *How: Ideas & Techniques in Graphic Design.* Networking with local graphic artists and joining business organizations also help you to become aware of community and national business trends.

Now that you've mapped out your business environment and are ready to approach clients with your work, it's time to answer the questions posed at the beginning of this chapter. Marketing and self-promotion are the key ingredients to a successful creative career. They're your way of letting the public know you exist and what product you're selling—your way of landing the assignments you seek. Marketing and self-promotion might well be the most creative challenge you'll encounter.

CHAPTER ONE CHECKLISTS

Freelance Market Opportunities

Markets you can contact by mail:
- [ ] magazine publishers
- [ ] greeting card publishers
- [ ] book publishers
- [ ] clip art firms
- [ ] art publishers and distributors

Markets you can contact either in person or by mail:
- [ ] newspaper publishers
- [ ] newsletter publishers
- [ ] associations
- [ ] institutions
- [ ] performing arts groups
- [ ] record companies
- [ ] syndicates

Markets you should usually contact in person:
- [ ] advertising agencies
- [ ] public relations firms
- [ ] art/design studios

Setting Up for Business

The minimum equipment you'll need to get started:
- [ ] a desk or large flat table
- [ ] file cabinet, file holders and labels
- [ ] bookcase
- [ ] storage rack or area
- [ ] good desk lamp
- [ ] index card box
- [ ] hardcover columnar record book or punched columnar pages with binder for record keeping
- [ ] accordion file or pocket folder

Optional equipment you can consider buying:
- [ ] personal computer
- [ ] photocopier
- [ ] separate business telephone
- [ ] phone answering machine
- [ ] bulletin board
- [ ] post office box

Keys to Maintaining Business

It will pay to continue increasing your business knowledge by:
- [ ] reading trade and business publications
- [ ] networking with artists
- [ ] joining organizations
- [ ] taking classes in business management
- [ ] contacting the Small Business Administration office in your area
- [ ] attending workshops on how to run a small business

Working From Your Studio

To work successfully from your own studio:
- [ ] Establish regular work hours
- [ ] Set times for coffee and meal breaks
- [ ] Arrange for child care, if necessary
- [ ] Develop a business attitude
- [ ] Take your business seriously
- [ ] Network with other artists
- [ ] Call in professionals to resolve complex business matters
- [ ] Create a businesslike environment in your studio or office
- [ ] Dress appropriately for business meetings
- [ ] Create a private work area
- [ ] Exercise regularly and eat regular, balanced meals

- [ ] Develop interests outside your work and art

Just as important as the things you should do, don't:
- [ ] Cut yourself off totally from outside stimulation
- [ ] Steal time from your work hours
- [ ] Allow family and friends to interrupt with nonemergency problems
- [ ] Become less concerned about your appearance
- [ ] Overeat
- [ ] Indulge in alcohol or drugs
- [ ] Be afraid to ask for respect and money for what you do
- [ ] Let your work consume your time for family
- [ ] Allow children to interfere with business meetings
- [ ] Think less of your business because it's at home

CHAPTER 2

MARKETING AND SELF-PROMOTION: THE ESSENTIALS

Every product and service you use has been marketed to you in some way—through print advertisements, TV commercials, a mailed flyer, or a personal sales contact. For a product to sell, its manufacturer must let you, the consumer, know it exists, how it meets your needs, why it's better than a similar product, and how and where you can buy it.

These are exactly the same steps to follow with *your* product—your talent and artwork—to realize its sale. Your consumers are the buyers of graphic art or design services. By doing research, developing a marketing plan, and creating the right marketing tools, you'll reach these buyers and sell your work.

NUTS AND BOLTS TERMINOLOGY

Let's begin our examination of marketing with some basic terms and abbreviations that might be unfamiliar if you haven't previously marketed your work.

Ad: Shortened term for advertisement and advertising.

AD and CD: Abbreviations for art director and creative director, respectively. These key people buy artwork from free-lancers, either in person or through the mail. Their responsibilities range, depending on the size of the firm, from total creative control of an entire project to a very limited power over only one aspect of a project, usually as a member of a creative *team*. They work directly with their firm's clients to understand the client's needs, and they retain free-lance artists and designers to supply the work that can't be handled in house. In some cases, there is no in-house art staff, and all work is free-lanced;

in other instances, a certain style or approach to a concept is desired, and a free-lancer is hired to supply it. This work can range from a single illustration to an entire art or design project. In small firms, the company president or the editor of a publication may handle the creative work without having an AD or CD title.

Assignment: Verbal or written information from an art director regarding art or design needs and deadlines for a specific project. The artist either accepts, rejects, or negotiates the AD's proposal. An artist who accepts the final terms assumes responsibility to fulfill the terms of the assignment agreement.

Client: The person or firm who hires the graphic artist to complete an assignment. Service-oriented companies such as ad agencies, PR firms and art or design studios have clients for whom they're producing the final product; thus you, as a graphic artist, are aiming to please *your* client, which is aiming to please *its* client.

Cold call: A phone call or visit to an AD or CD with whom you've had no previous contact.

Deadline: The agreed-upon date for submission of the completed assignment to the art/creative director (client).

Drop-off: Leaving your portfolio at the AD's office and picking it up following the director's review. No in-person interview takes place. (The pros and cons of drop-offs are discussed in Chapter 5.)

Graphic artist: An illustrator, designer, or pasteup artist who works under the direction of a supervisor or an art director for a specific commercial reason and receives payment for artwork at an agreed-upon rate and time, usually at the completion of the assignment.

Marketing field or area: The graphic art area(s), such as publishing or advertising, on which the artist chooses to focus. Also known as a **target market.**

Marketing tools: Samples and printed materials that aid the graphic artist in contacting potential clients and advertising and selling his work. (These are discussed at length in Chapter 3.)

Over the transom: The purchase and use by an art director of a sample (usually an illustration or cartoon) that a graphic artist has submitted through his portfolio or mailing package, rather than having one created specifically by assignment. Over the transom purchases don't happen frequently, but are most likely to occur in the magazine, newspaper and greeting card industries.

PR firms: Abbreviation for public relations firms. These firms differ from advertising agencies which communicate to the public information regarding a single product or event. PR firms assume responsibility for creating communication about an organization, corporation, business or institution. This communication can involve promotion, public affairs, publicity, advertising, marketing and press agency.

Presentation: An all-inclusive term for the display of your artwork, your information, and yourself to a prospective client. Usually used exclusively in relation to inperson client meetings.

SASE: Abbreviation for self-addressed stamped envelope.

Simultaneous submissions: Examples of artwork offered at the same time to more than one firm. Usually refers exclusively to mail submissions.

CANDID RETROSPECTION

Norman Adams was a full-time free-lance illustrator for ten years and is now an art director with Sheehy & Knopf advertising agency in Louisville, Kentucky. He candidly reveals that in looking back over his free-lance career he sees some major mistakes in underestimating the importance of marketing and continuity of effort.

"For my marketing efforts, I sent out flyers and I placed some quarter-page ads in publications, but I didn't do it successfully, probably because I didn't saturate the market. Saturation is a big point to consider. The more you're out there, the more they know you. It's public relations; you run your own public relations office for *you* the supplier, the illustrator, the artist, the designer, whatever.

"The flyer was sent out as a cold call to a list of art directors, creative directors, art buyers, anyone I thought would be interested in seeing what I had to offer. Then I'd follow that up with some different pieces. If I didn't get a call or some kind of recognition after the second or third time, I'd take them off the list.

"I didn't strategically plan my marketing, and now that I'm in the agency, I see a good use for marketing strategy and a schedule. As a free-lancer, I saw advertising, I saw marketing, I saw public relations, but I didn't tie them together—I didn't see the *need* to tie them together. It's hard for me to say that, because I *should* have seen it. It's so simple, so true, that all

MARKETING: WHAT IS IT, AND HOW DO YOU DO IT?

Any marketing effort has the goal

three should work together.

"I didn't pursue marketing and self-promotion. I thought if I got something out, it's good, it'll help. But in reality, I should have had more of a strategy.

"Take my Sis! Boom! Baa! mailer, for example, shown right. I was completely thrilled with that piece. I thought it made total sense. It said that I was an illustrator because I illustrated each of the words, then creatively handled it by tying the words *A Norman Adams illustration is something to cheer about* into the Sis! Boom! Baa! headline. I felt that it was just a great piece. I ran it in the *Creative Black Book,* and no one called. I didn't do enough with it. I should have followed it up with another piece. I didn't have a strategy, and it just fell apart.

"This mailer was effective when I was job hunting because I did more with it. I used it as the cover to the resume (see page 56) that explained who I was, my background, and what I wanted to do, and contained several other pieces I'd done. Three weeks after mailing out my resumes, I'd send the same Sis! Boom! Baa! mailer with a note, 'Did you receive my resume?' Art directors remembered the card as the cover of my resume; the piece finally got the recognition I thought it deserved, and I got calls.

"Maybe this is the key: when I was job hunting, I didn't see this piece as a tool, rather as a necessity—I wanted a job. But maybe that's how you have to view every potential assignment—as a job, a necessity—and use your promotional pieces with this attitude."

A NORMAN ADAMS ILLUSTRATION IS SOMETHING TO CHEER ABOUT.

3816 Warner Avenue, Louisville, KY 40207
RSVP answering service (212) 857-9267
(502) 895-4513

Norman Adams advises artists to view their promotional pieces, such as his mailer, as necessities, whose various uses should be maximized.

stated at the beginning of this chapter: to inform the consumer of the product's existence, of how it meets his needs and where it can be purchased.

There is a specific marketing strategem you can use to sell your work and services most directly and economically. Read these steps carefully: they're vital to your overall success.

- Analyze your product.
- Find its appropriate market area.
- Locate potential clients within

that market area.
- Establish a marketing strategy.
- Develop a marketing plan.
- Evaluate and update your marketing efforts.

Your marketing efforts need to be well plotted and refined in order to reach the buyers who are *most likely* to want and need your product. And you should consistently continue your endeavors so that your name and work stay fresh in art directors' minds.

In this chapter we'll consider the first two points on the road to achieving your goals. Later chapters will discuss the rest of the steps. The sidebar, Candid Retrospection, pages 20 and 21, presents sound advice from a successful free-lancer turned art director about how—and how not—to market.

IDENTIFYING YOUR PRODUCT'S STRENGTHS AND WEAKNESSES

The first step on the way to reaching your marketing goals is to evaluate the assets and limitations of your artwork. Since the ultimate aim is to match product qualities with client needs, you must understand your product inside and out, strengths and weaknesses alike, so that you know what you're selling. Without this knowledge, you'll never decisively narrow your marketing endeavors to the general target area where your work fits most naturally, to the appropriate outlets within that area, and then to specific potential clients.

View your work objectively; be honest with yourself. By listing its strengths, you gain a clearer picture of its marketing assets, its strongest selling points. By identifying its weaknesses, you can evaluate whether you need to sharpen or

change some skills to make your work more marketable or to leave it as it is and restrict yourself to the market areas that will respond to it.

Select a group of your works—illustrations, cartoons, greeting cards, catalog designs, whatever it is that you do and that you wish to sell—and answer the following questions about them. Before you write or tape your answers, think at length about those qualities of your art or design that prompt your responses. Consider the questions in detail, and draft your responses as clearly and descriptively as you can. (*Note:* Your answers to the questions about the strong points of your work will later form the basis for the written text in your marketing and promotional tools.) Again, remember to be objective. Evaluate what your art, *on its own merit,* says to you—not what you *hope* it says.

1. How does your technique add depth and character to the subjects?
2. How do your finished pieces show an understanding of and skill with your medium?
3. How would you describe your personal style? What elements separate it from other work in the same medium or on the same theme?
4. What three characteristics of your style will attract art buyers to your work ahead of the work of others?
5. What facets of your style are most ideally suited to carrying a client's message?
6. What characteristics of your medium and of your style make it suitable for reproduction in color? in black and white?

7. How does your work show a creative, expressive, or effective use of typography? of color?
8. What elements of your art or design are most eye-catching, and why? Which are surprising, and why? Which are amusing, and why?
9. Viewing each piece of art before you as the result of a specific assignment, whether self- or client-generated, explain how each piece fulfilled the project's original concept.
10. What about your work pulls together all the diverse elements in each piece into a harmoniously balanced whole?
11. Given your style and the techniques and media with which you prefer to work, what subject matters will you be most capable of illustrating, and how can you vary your style, techniques, and media to meet the fullest range of client needs?
12. How much of its intended message does each work convey to the viewer? What else would you be likely to add if you were standing beside that viewer "listening" to your work? How could you incorporate your remarks more clearly into your artwork?
13. In each piece of your artwork or design, how have you captured the spirit of the subject as well as the image?
14. Looking at the separate pieces of art or design as one body of work, describe its level of consistent quality.

Keeping the same group of pieces before you, examine your creative weaknesses. Remember that it's okay to have the weaknesses and that the first step in neutralizing their negative effects and eventually turning them to strengths is identifying them. Answer these questions as honestly and fully as you did the previous ones.

1. What aspects of your style are not well suited to reproduction in print?
2. How is your technique or medium too delicate or too heavy to reproduce well on a small scale? on a large scale? in color? in black and white?
3. In this group of art or design pieces, how many different subject matters have you illustrated? In which subject area does your best work seem to concentrate, and how might this concentration hinder you from taking on a variety of assignments?
4. In what ways have you employed the same design solutions for a range of different design problems, and to what extent has monotony settled over the body of your artwork?
5. Considering the samples of your art and design before you, in which medium are you least proficient and in what ways does this lack of skill show itself in your work? With what techniques are you less adept, and how could you change your style to minimize this weakness?
6. What elements in your pieces are going to make them look dated in a year? Which pieces are faddish and contrived, and what elements are responsible for this?

7. Looking at those works in which typography is an element, how does the design or the illustration portion overpower the type and hide the message?
8. If any of your finished pieces have not fulfilled the original project's intention, how have they failed, and how could they have been improved?

The information you have just compiled in your art analysis is quite valuable to your work as an artist and as a marketer. Don't think, "Good, that's done!" and put it out of sight and mind. Use it to see yourself and your art more clearly and to get a firm idea of what you can and can't supply to the marketplace. Repeat the analysis periodically throughout your work life with different pieces to prompt consistent fine tuning of your marketing efforts.

FINDING THE RIGHT MARKET FOR YOUR PRODUCT

The next important question is what do you enjoy doing? This question is especially important if you work in a variety of media and subject areas or if you use a diversity of skills.

The illustration market areas suitable to the medium, technique, and subject you prefer and the design market areas most likely to offer the projects you find exciting are the ones to try first. You should not exclude other market areas, because no assignment lasts forever, but it's ridiculous to market your work continuously in areas that provide assignments you don't really enjoy. Start with the ones that will bring you the greatest satisfaction, challenge, growth—and enjoyment. If these don't work out, then you can re-evaluate and, if necessary, compromise.

Self-examination and research are the primary ingredients for finding the appropriate market area(s) for your work. (Remember, we're still referring to general marketing areas or fields, such as publishing or advertising.) If you're an artist who's had one area in mind for a long time and have been refining your skill and research to this market over a period of years, this step isn't currently necessary for you. But if you've simply enjoyed "drawing" or are so diverse you aren't sure where you belong, now's the time to determine which areas to approach.

Though all types of art and design are suitable at one time or another in all markets, some market areas lend themselves more readily to your style, medium, subject matter, and design than do others. To isolate those areas, ask yourself the following questions:

1. Where have I seen printed types of work similar to mine? As greeting cards? Magazine illustrations? Record album covers?
2. Is my design ability more suited to small businesses with less complex needs, or to large corporations with a wide variety of sophisticated projects?
3. Can I find potential buyers for my work nationwide or is it better to remain local?
4. If I should remain local, do I live in a metropolitan area large enough to support me through assignments in my preferred field?
5. If I like a variety of assignments, is it more to my benefit to approach a service-oriented marketing field that deals with a range of clients? Or is my work best

suited to a field limited to one type of product?

As an example, let's follow Janet Crane as she goes through this process of choosing a market field. Her subject matter is diverse, but her illustration style is strong, black-and-white cartoon and caricature drawings. She knows many market areas use this type of drawing from time to time, but at this stage in the development of her marketing plan, she wants to focus on the ones *most* open to using her work. She asks herself, Where have I seen a cartoon-style illustration most often? Magazines, of course; some newspapers, greeting cards, advertisements. To a lesser degree she's found this style in books, particularly juvenile and adult humor, audiovisual materials such as slide shows and film strips, record covers, prints and posters, and miscellaneous materials such as flyers, brochures and catalogs produced by public relations firms, small businesses, associations, institutions, and art or design studios. She's seldom seen them in the architectural, interior or landscape design, fashion, or performing arts fields. The town she lives in supports only two advertising agencies, no publishing firms except for one local morning newspaper, and no large institutions with public-relations budgets. There are quite a few small businesses, especially tourist shops. Crane prefers to market her work in person so she decides to cultivate the small businesses as clients. Her other high-use marketing areas—magazines, ad agencies, greeting card companies—she'll approach by mail.

So Crane's narrowed her focus to four target areas, possibly five. She won't forget the others; she'll merely direct her attention first to those most open to her type of work.

Crane next narrows these areas down even more to concentrate her marketing efforts and tools. She examines her personality, work methods and medium, and her present knowledge of the various fields.

You can do this, too, if you find yourself with several marketing areas where your work seems to be appropriate. Ask yourself:

1. Do I "lean" to one area more than another—possess a natural interest in a specific field?
2. Do I create work overnight or prefer to spend several days working out a concept or studying a particular subject?
3. Do I prefer to rough out numerous sketches before selecting the one to finish, or am I pretty much of a "quick study" graphic artist?
4. Am I turned off by chaos and pressure under which some firms, such as advertising agencies, frequently work? Or is it vice versa, with my excitement stemming both from the deadline pressure and the visual prominence that art and design command in ads?
5. Does my medium allow me to meet tight deadlines or, like the oil painter who produces full-color magazine cover illustrations, do I need weeks until my work can be given to a client?
6. How much time am I planning to devote to my art—full-time, part-time, or only occasional effort?
7. If I'm only working part-time or occasionally, does this restrict me in the assignments I can accept from some of these markets

and therefore make them less profitable to solicit?

You know yourself better than anyone, and only you can decide the market area in which you think you'll most enjoy assignments. If all of the areas seem equally desirable to you at this point, select one that offers the most outlets; for example, there are many more magazines than greeting card publishers and newspapers.

Janet Crane realizes that she'll have to do some solicitation through the mail because of where she lives, and she has chosen to focus on magazines because they are numerous. In person she'll approach the local businesses. These two groups are now Crane's high-priority marketing areas. Secondary areas are book publishers for mail solicitation and small ad agencies in the city nearest her for in-person contacts.

SELF-PROMOTION: THE ART OF BLOWING YOUR OWN HORN

Self-promotion and marketing are two sides of the same coin and difficult to separate most of the time. But self-promotion, the ongoing process of building name recognition and reputation, isn't necessarily tied into the actual marketing of your work. In self-promotion, you're identifying and establishing yourself as a graphic artist, not only to potential clients, but to the community as well. You're letting everyone, whether potential art buyers or not, know who you are and what you do. In essence, you're blowing your own horn whenever and wherever you tactfully can do so.

Graphic art is a people business. The more people you know, the more people you talk to, the more you increase your chances of getting an assignment. Relatives, friends, neighbors—all have other contacts who just might own a retail or service company or be involved in public relations, publishing, advertising. If *your* contacts don't know you are a graphic artist and the type of work you do, they can't recommend you to *their* contacts. Many contacts are social ones to begin with, so *always* carry your business card with you. Don't be afraid in a social setting to say who you are and what you do. You have to get the word around.

Self-promotional efforts, therefore, should be well thought out, but not necessarily as refined and strategic as marketing efforts. Generally you're letting everyone know of your abilities and interests, not just clients who are likely to buy your work.

You'll find further discussion of self-promotion in Chapter 5, where networking, volunteerism, mailings, organization membership, lecturing, and advertising are covered.

In the sidebar beginning on page 27, one designer talks about getting started as a free-lancer, selecting a field of work, putting together marketing materials for herself, and handling one client's promotional campaign.

MARKETING AND VISUAL COMMUNICATION

Sue Crolick began her one-person ad agency, Sue T. Crolick Advertising and Design, four years ago, encountering firsthand many of the problems creative people face when attempting to market their work. Despite twenty-three years as an advertising art director and designer, her first self-promotion/marketing campaign was unsuccessful.

"When I started my own agency, trying to determine my exact market was very difficult for me because I was getting business from all areas. Because I had no specialty, the world was my market. It's very hard to know how to talk to or send mailers to or create ads for the world. I had to narrow my field."

Crolick analyzed her skills and desires and focused her client field to specialize in marketing creative people to creative people. She now designs logos, ad campaigns, and direct-mail pieces for film companies, musicians, photographers, artists' reps, printers, and other creative-service firms.

Her unique position as an art director, a creator of advertising directed *to* art directors and an independent business person going after her own clients provides an understanding of all aspects of marketing and self-promotion. From her office in Minneapolis she discusses what she considers typical difficulties freelancers face:

"One thing that's hard to do, especially when you're starting out, is to think of yourself as a product. Good marketing requires the ability to distance yourself—what you do—from your personal self. Most people are too self-conscious to do that.

"I think we creative people are often shy and have more difficulty selling ourselves because as a group we generally tend to be introverted and introspective. Selling takes an aggressiveness and assertiveness many of us don't have. But you have to push yourself out there, and it does get easier the more you do it.

"I also think it's important to have a specialty, to find your niche. The most successful marketing comes about when you have a very clear idea not only of what you do, but also of what you don't do. It's much easier to remember someone who does a particular thing than someone who does a little bit of everything. You also need a clear idea of exactly who buys what you do, precisely who your audience is.

"Most graphic creators, especially when they're starting out, don't have a budget that allows them to promote to a lot of people. By finding your specialty, you narrow down what you do and more readily target whom you want to contact. Then your communication is more effective because it's pointed and specific. You're also able to deal realistically with your budget because you're not marketing to *everyone* out there.

She observes, however, that "marketing yourself has an air of unreality about it. There's no deadline except for the one you set for yourself, nobody's paying you to do it and you can't immediately see a direct benefit. All of these factors make the whole process seem not very real. To counteract these feelings, you have to make self-promotion a real *assignment* for yourself so that you plan it out and are consistent."

When designing a client's campaign, Crolick knows the value of communication and how to take advantage of every opportunity.

"Wherever there's graphic design, there's an opportunity to get an idea across. You can do more than just decorate; you can send a real message. The letterhead is a classic case—people tend to think of it only as decoration, but often it's a missed opportunity to get an idea across about yourself. I've even used written copy in letterheads. Think

The four-part logo on Sue Crolick's letterhead, envelope, and business card exhibits her skill as a visual communicator. Breaking her name into four syllables she illustrated each with a visual homonym. For all of her stationery she's chosen a beige stock printed in green, orange and rust. Crolick has rearranged the graphic and type elements on all three pieces to fit the proportions of each. The name-address-phone line appears at the foot of the letterhead, running vertically up the side of the envelope, and broken into two units enclosing the graphic on the business card. The four-part graphic is stacked on the left end of her envelope and positioned horizontally on letterhead and card. For a label on oversized envelopes and finished art Crolick uses her business card design printed on self-adhesive white coated stock.

© Sue Crolick. Used with permission.

of it as an advertisement for yourself."

Crolick's own company letterhead and accompanying stationery materials illustrate her belief that graphic artists can be visual communicators by what they do with their logos. Her visual word play with her name creates a mnemonic device to "help people remember me. That's such a basic principle of marketing—to get people to remember you."

But she admits there is one thing she would do differently if redesigning it— select a larger typeface to make her name more readable.

"I was bent on having my stationery tasteful, wanting to downplay the Sioux Tea Crow Lick so that it didn't turn out to be cornball. So I thought I'd select restrained color and small type. Now when people start fumbling for their glasses to read it, I realize that was not a good thing to do. Design for people over forty—type is there for communication."

When creating promotional pieces for her clients, Sue uses an approach more indicative of her advertising than her graphic design background.

"The first thing I determine is my mes-

Crolick's packet of printed marketing and promotional materials for keyliner Nancy Johnson carries the same message consistently placed throughout. A clever headline, strong black type and the simple thumb-smudge graphic to push home the visual pun appear on her letterhead, envelope, self-adhesive mailing and mechanical label, business card, single-ply invoice, and cardstock mailer. All pieces are printed in black on bright white stock. The straightforward message and design prove Crolick's claim that she strips away "everything that doesn't directly contribute to getting the idea across."

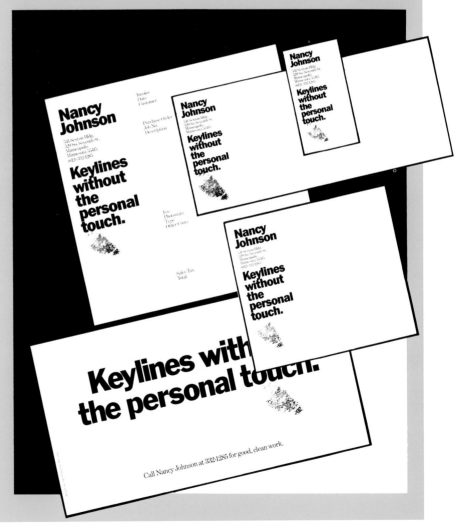

sage: What am I trying to get across? Then everything I design is keyed directly to that message. I don't do anything that is purely decorative; there's nothing extraneous. I strip away everything that doesn't directly contribute to getting that idea across. It's a form of editing that I apply to everything I do."

When designing a marketing campaign for keyline artist Nancy Johnson, Crolick was familiar both with the client and the market she was approaching. She had purchased Johnson's paste-up/production services for years and knew exactly what the artist did; since Johnson's market is art directors, Crolick felt right at home. The challenge was to communicate to other art directors Johnson's skills; Crolick chose to play on the theme of what a keyliner *shouldn't* do.

"Often the most interesting angle in any problem is the negative. This area often seems more human; it has possibilities for entertainment and humor. You demonstrate how good you are by showing what you're not. The trick is to do it in such a way that the positive ultimately comes through. As an art director I knew all the intricacies and specifics of keylining mistakes, so whenever possible I went for an idea that demonstrated that problem.

"I had such a limited budget with Nancy's campaign that there was no money for a copywriter. Necessity being the mother of invention, I discovered I could actually write body copy, which was a new experience for me. I had written headlines before, but this was a new stretch for me personally. Sometimes having a very tight budget can increase your creativity. You have such narrow parameters to work in that you have to think more cleverly, more freshly. You might even surprise yourself with what you can do."

Johnson's ad campaign was a huge success, turning a business slump into a business turnaround.

"We sent out a card, and people noticed it and hung it up and got a chuckle out of it. Then people started calling, and her business picked up. Nancy is a perfect example of someone whose work is so good, all she had to do is let people know she's here. She just needed to make some noise."

Nancy Johnson agrees that the campaign pieces caught art directors' attention, and client calls followed.

"These have been just wonderful pieces for me. I mail a card out about every one to three months and can tell they've communicated well because my business has improved a lot. I've even received calls from other keyliners telling me that the pieces are great and that they can really identify with them.

"I think it was a very good business decision on my part because I'm in business by myself and, when mailed, these pieces act as my representative. I purchased a mailing list from a private mailing list business so that I can solicit the art directors, the designers, and all the different categories of people I want to reach.

"My market is Minneapolis because of the nature of my work. A lot of times my jobs only require half an hour of work and the client wants it back as soon as possible. So I mail the cards to people in downtown Minneapolis where my studio is located. This allows me to reach close potential clients and offer service within the time limit they want.

"This limitation is one of the things Sue and I thought about a lot. We really isolated the clients I wanted to reach and geared the ideas of the cards to those people. The cards are entertaining for the people receiving them and stand out from all the other mail they get."

The campaign has been a success for Crolick as well as Johnson, gathering a variety of kudos, including awards from the New York Art Directors Club, the Minneapolis Advertising Show, and the Minnesota Graphic Designers Associa-

Sometimes, you don't find out you hired the wrong keyliner until it's too late. until it's too late.

What good is a new line of type if the old line is still there?
Trust your corrections to a keyliner who does more than paste up type proofs. She *reads* type proofs.
Nancy Johnson, Keyliner 332-1285

Sometimes, you don't find out you hired the wrong keyliner until it's too la

When an ad runs, the wrong crop marks could mean disaster. Copywriters could discover their headlines are suddenly short. Art directors could find their pictures in the gutter.

The safe thing to do is hire a keyliner who knows her live area from her bleed: Nancy Johnson.

She'll check and re-check every measurement, to guarantee you accuracy. With no unfortunate surprises.

Remember: whoever said, "Great advertising knows no boundaries," wasn't talking about the keyline.
Nancy Johnson, Keyliner, Downtown Minneapolis 332-1285

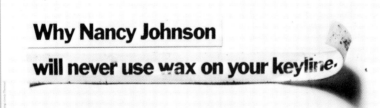

Why Nancy Johnson will never use wax on your keyline.

First, because wax doesn't stick for very long. Which means if your keyline is around for more than a week, your headline might not be.

Second, because wax tends to turn yellow. So an ad that hasn't run yet can look like it already ran.

If you want a keyline that lasts, call Nancy Johnson.

She uses 2-coat cement, which gives you the best possible bond. And, unlike wax, it leaves no residue.

Remember: when Nancy Johnson keylines your ad, she wants your *idea* to come off. Not your type.

Nancy Johnson, Keyliner, Downtown Mpls. 332-1285

Focusing on keyliners' weaknesses, Crolick designed a clever series of mailers, shown on the next three pages, to point up Johnson's strengths. She supported her no-nonsense headlines with visual examples of the mistakes she decried. Johnson self-mails the 6″ × 11″ cardstock pieces every couple of months to clients and prospects and has experienced a large upsurge in business since the mail campaign began.

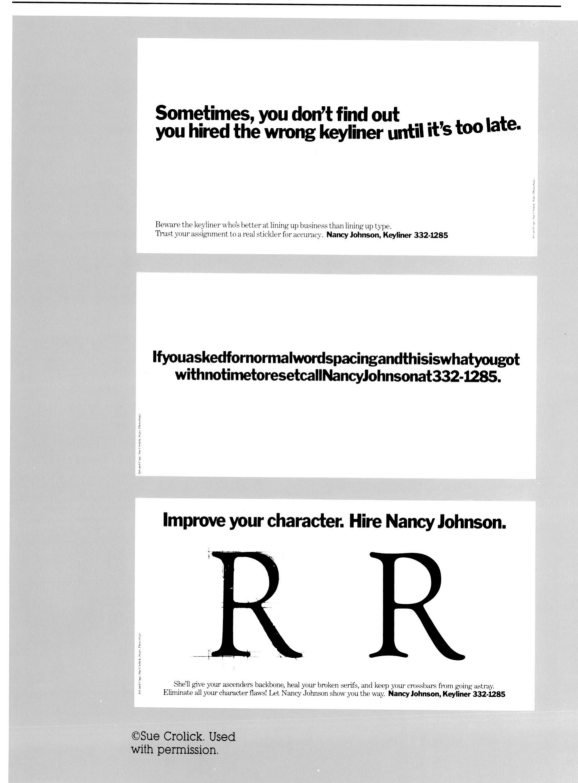

Sometimes, you don't find out you hired the wrong keyliner until it's too late.

Beware the keyliner who's better at lining up business than lining up type.
Trust your assignment to a real stickler for accuracy. **Nancy Johnson, Keyliner 332-1285**

Ifyouaskedfornormalwordspacingandthisiswhatyougot withnotimetoresetcallNancyJohnsonat332-1285.

Improve your character. Hire Nancy Johnson.

She'll give your ascenders backbone, heal your broken serifs, and keep your crossbars from going astray.
Eliminate all your character flaws! Let Nancy Johnson show you the way. **Nancy Johnson, Keyliner 332-1285**

Is your keyliner editing the c py?

Art and Copy: Sue Crolick, Stats. Photo/Stats, Retouching: Gordy Thorstad

It's one thing to lose a great headline because the client didn't like it.

It's another thing to lose it because it fell off the keyline.

For type that sticks, call Nancy Johnson. She uses 2-coat cement, to give the best possible bond.

And, instead of simply pasting type corrections on top, she cuts a mortise.

So even a one-letter change stays firmly in place. Remember: when Nancy Johnson keylines your ad, she wants your *idea* to come off. Not your type.

Nancy Johnson, Keyliner. Phone 332-1285

tion.

Crolick offers two additional points she considers important for free-lancers marketing and promoting themselves:

"The first one is the reminder principle; it's so important to stay top-of-mind and to continue to remind people that you're here. McDonald's has sold billions of hamburgers and yet continues to make new commercials. They do that because they know if you don't keep reminding people you're here, they're going to forget you. In this modern world where we're inundated constantly with images and messages, communication and advertising, we have to pay attention to the tune-out factor.

"Spread out your budget so that each marketing piece is less expensive, but you have enough to be able to remind people you're around for possibly six months to a year. Sometimes free-lancers put a lot of money into one smashing piece or one huge six-color poster. It's far better to do a continuing campaign with a number of less expensive pieces.

"Second is the entertainment principle. I believe you have a much better chance of penetrating and leaving a good impression if you are fast and entertaining with what you do.

"Learn to empathize. In advertising you must develop a keen sensitivity for others. Art directors have very little time; they're busy and harried, and you're interrupting with your advertisement. Learn to do that in the most persuasive and pleasing way, giving them something for their time.

"Humor is a wonderful way to do that. A laugh makes you feel good. If you can give your audience a good feeling, a moment of fun, for the time they're giving you, it's more of an even trade. When you give somebody a chuckle or a laugh, it's like giving them a little present."

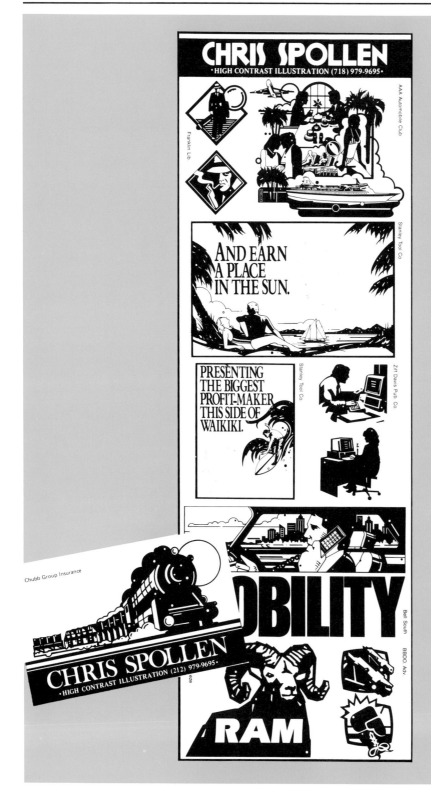

Clever layout, careful scoring, and accordion folding turn Chris Spollen's long b/w flyer into an oversized "matchbook" full of his high-contrast graphics. Each page of the fold reveals an illustration and a client name. The bottom cover flap has his name, specialty, and phone number in strong type reversed out of a solid black background. The folded format offers the greatest economy of space, allowing illustrations to be placed very close together but viewed separately.

CHAPTER TWO
CHECKLISTS

Steps to Successful Marketing

Marketing of your art or design should follow in an organized order:
- [ ] Remember the basic principle: get people to remember you
- [ ] Think of self and work as products
- [ ] Analyze your products' strengths and weaknesses
- [ ] Maintain a clear idea of what you do and don't do
- [ ] Locate appropriate market areas
- [ ] Locate potential clients
- [ ] Know your specialty and audience
- [ ] Establish marketing strategy
- [ ] Strive for pointed and specific communication
- [ ] Develop marketing plan
- [ ] Make marketing and self-promotion a planned, consistent self-assignment
- [ ] Evaluate and update your marketing efforts

Product Strengths

The more your art or design satisfies the following list, the stronger your product:
- [ ] Technique adds depth and character to subject matter
- [ ] Exhibits understanding of and skill with the medium
- [ ] Communicates a developed personal style
- [ ] Style delivers client's message
- [ ] Medium and style suitable for print reproduction
- [ ] Exhibits creative and effective use of typography and color
- [ ] Contains eye-catching elements
- [ ] Fulfills project's concept and needs
- [ ] Diverse elements are unified, balanced and harmonious
- [ ] Meets fullest range of client needs possible
- [ ] Spirit of subject captured as well as image
- [ ] Body of work shows consistent quality

Product Weaknesses

Your weaknesses are evident if:
- [ ] Style, technique or medium unsuited to print reproduction
- [ ] Subject matter too narrow for numerous assignments
- [ ] Works are monotonous
- [ ] Lack of skill is evident
- [ ] Works appear outdated, faddish or contrived
- [ ] Lack of harmony between illustration and typography
- [ ] Failure to fulfill project's concept

Finding the Right Market Area

To locate the best market for your art or design:
- [ ] Determine where similar types of works are reproduced
- [ ] Distinguish between simple versus complex client needs
- [ ] Distinguish between needs of local versus national clients
- [ ] Ascertain ability of local area to support your career
- [ ] Determine your work's suitability to variety of assignments
- [ ] Analyze direction of your artistic interests
- [ ] Understand artistic methods of working
- [ ] Determine amount of time you want to devote to your career

CHAPTER 3

TOOLS OF THE TRADE

You're familiar with the tools you need to produce your artwork—the knives, inks, pens, paints, markers. This chapter will familiarize you with other vital tools—the ones needed to communicate your professional business image *and* your art to potential buyers. These are the tools that allow you to put your marketing and self-promotional strategies into action. Pick and choose from them as finances allow and needs arise, but always aim toward a marketing and self-promotional package that communicates a rich talent, a knowledge of art skills, and a strong business sense.

Evaluate each item offered here in terms of your long- and short-range goals, your marketing field, potential clients, methods of contact. Create a design element that carries through all your materials—a logo, distinctive use of border striping, color combination, etc.—before you begin to produce specific pieces. With this consistent element in place, the basic "look" of your materials pulls them together and provides a unified package, no matter how many or how few pieces are included for a particular client. Multiple uses can be made of a single piece by offering it alone or in conjunction with other marketing and promotional materials.

You must make a firm financial commitment to the production of these materials. They are acting as your spokesperson when you're not around and must present you and your work in a manner that's interesting, exciting, and professional. As you're budgeting your money month by month so that the "fat" months cover the expenses of the "lean" ones, allocate a definite amount for the production of marketing and self-promotional materials. The actual amount will be determined by your income and the types of materials you're planning.

Let's begin with those most important communicators of your illustration style, technique, medium, subject matter, and design ability—your art/design samples.

ART SAMPLES

Samples of your work fall into two broad categories, reproductions and original works, and are what you present to clients in person in a portfolio or through the mail in a mailing package. Their purpose is to show the potential client what you do and how you do it, the range of your talent and experience, and the type of work you'd like to create for him or her.

Your first task is to determine which sample type(s) best display your work. In light of their importance, sample(s) should be the one(s) most suited to your medium and method of client contact and the *very* best your finances allow. You can select more than one type of sample depending on the method of contact, the type of work you do, and whether the samples are to be returned or filed.

There are five types of samples:

- Slides and transparencies
- Photographs
- Photostats
- Photocopies
- Original works

The first four are reproductions of your work; the fifth includes actual printed final products, such as brochures and magazine ads (known as tear sheets) and original design work or illustrations.

Slides and Transparencies

Slides and transparencies are actually one and the same: A transparency is a *positive* film image (as opposed to a negative image that's used for photographic prints) that varies in size according to the film size used. A slide is a transparency mounted in a sturdy frame, more commonly called a slide mount.

The transparency size most commonly used for art samples is made with 35mm film and called, obviously, a 35mm slide. Slides can be used as samples in either a portfolio or a mailed submission. Depending on the number you send and your finances, you can request that the prospective client return them or keep them on file.

Slides are small, light, easy to han-

JEAN MILLER RN.,B.R.(fine arts), Hon B.Sc.A.R.M.,R.M.I.
MEDICAL ILLUSTRATOR   TEL. (416) 883-4114

Jean Miller's photographed sample combines four-color illustration and black type on one photographic print. Miller is a Toronto medical illustrator.

dle, relatively inexpensive, good communicators of color and of your ability to handle your medium. They're ideal for generating a sequential slide program—a series of pictures that in themselves give an overview of a particular work or project. For example, if you have designed and illustrated a magazine ad for a previous client, you can supply a slide each of the thumbnails, rough sketch, comprehensive, original illustration, a detail slide showing a close-up section of the illustration, and a final slide showing the printed ad. This type of series provides the current art director insight into your creative thinking processes and proves your ability to handle a project from beginning to end.

The greatest disadvantage to slides is that an art director must use some kind of viewing apparatus in order to get their full impact. Most but not all creative departments have a projector and at least a clear wall, if not an actual screen, available. The art director, however, must be motivated enough to use them. This isn't as great an issue during an in-person review as it is with a mailed submission.

Other apparatus used for viewing slides are hand-held viewers, light tables, and overhead lights, listed in descending order of desirability. Some models of hand-held viewers provide modest magnification; others merely illuminate the slide from behind. Invest in a viewer that has both capabilities. If you're taking slides to an in-person review, you're prepared in case the art director has only a light table available or the projector is broken. This type of viewer is also invaluable for reviewing and editing your slides at home.

A light table (a table or movable box with a light source shining through a plastic or glass top) doesn't magnify your slides; they can be viewed, but detail and impact are lost.

Then there is the old "hold them up to the light and see if anything interests me" tactic. This does the least to reveal anything good about your work, but everyone does it, and art directors are no exception.

As an art director, Norman Adams receives numerous mailing packages containing slides and his viewing of them covers the entire range or methods:

"Usually I'll put the slides on the light table; sometimes I just hold them up to an overhead light. If I'm excited by some of them or if there's something there other than what I'm seeing all the time, then I'll put them on the projector. But I often do put them on the projector because I like to explore new things. Even if it's bad, I like to look at it, examine it, and try to determine what the artist was thinking when he drew it."

Because you can never be sure in what manner your slides will be viewed, each slide must be the best attainable photograph of your work.

A "good" slide possesses these qualities:

- It's color-true—the slide's reproduced color matches the color in your original work.
- The photographed work fills the film frame, the image area of the slide. If the artwork is not proportional to the slide's image area, it should be centered with equal amounts of space top and bottom and even amounts of space on each side.
- No distracting articles or printed background fabrics are in the frame. These draw attention

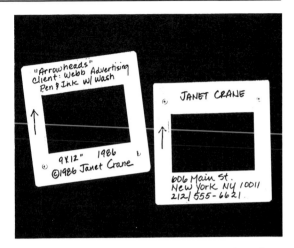

This typical slide has been labeled by hand utilizing white self-adhesive labels cut into strips to fit the slide mount. Labeling puts all pertinent information at the art director's fingertips, orients the slide for right-side-up insertion into a projector, and indicates ownership should it be separated from the rest of your materials. The top slide shows the front; the bottom slide, the back.

away from the work. "Sweeps," large rolls of background paper in black or a neutral tone with little hue are available at most photography and some art-supply stores. They provide a clean background and are easily rerolled and stored until the next use. Velvet black is a favorite with many photographers, but select the color most appropriate to your work. The work should stand out from the background. Dark subjects shouldn't be photographed on black; rather, select a neutral value within the subject and match the background to it.

- The edges of the photographed work are straight and centered. If a work is photographed off-center, special photographic masking tape (available at photography stores) can be applied to the slide to cut out unwanted background areas; only the desired image is then projected. Because it's time-consuming to mask each slide and unsightly in a slide sheet you're wiser to be sure the work is photographed properly at the outset.

- The photographed work is in focus and sharp.
- No glare or "hot spots" due to improper lighting cause blank white areas on the work.

Always own duplicate slides; make them yourself or have them made through a photography lab. They're necessary for multiple slide portfolios or mailing packages and to keep a record at your studio of the work you've done. If you're doing your own photography and feel *very* comfortable with your skills, duplicate slides can be made by shooting the same piece of artwork over and over again as many times as you need slides. These are not true duplicates as photography labs think of them, because each slide is actually an "original" shot. These "duplicates" supply greater clarity and are more color-true than lab-produced duplicates. A *word of caution:* If a mistake is made on the first shot, that error is repeated on each slide.

If a photography lab is making your dupes, it takes your one "original" slide and in essence rephotographs it using special slide film, lights, and so on. There can be a loss of sharpness and contrast and possibly a slight shift in color balance. No such duplicate is as good as the original, but the better the lab, the closer the match. Therefore, you want to find the *best* lab.

Take time to research the labs in your area before handing over your

These are slide sheets, one empty (left) and the other filled with 20 slides ready for labeling. Sheets like these keep your slides clean, in order, and can be placed in a three-ring or toothed notebook. They promote easy editing of the slides for a portfolio presentation. Clear vinyl allows viewing of the entire sheet on a light table without removing them from the protective wrap.

precious samples. Ask other artists what they did and didn't like about duplicates they have received. Photography store salespeople who specialize in selling cameras and equipment sometimes will provide recommendations; ask if they're based on personal experience. Talk to the lab personnel; explain your need for clarity and accurate color and gauge their interest and expertise through their responses. Get price quotes—cheaper is not necessarily the way to go with samples, but labs have quantity cutoff points where prices change. You might be further ahead to get fifty slides instead of the twenty-five you originally estimated *if* you will use them. Ask to see previous work to see how closely they approximated an original slide. Lacking such samples, ask for a referral to a previous artist-customer.

All slides should be labeled; slides destined for an art director's file or mailing packages *must* be labeled. Labeling not only provides immediate identification should the slide be separated from the rest of your materials, but also supplies pertinent information regarding the photographed work. On the front of the slide mount (the side facing you when the art is correctly oriented) print a brief one- or two-word description or title, client (if applicable), medium, size of the photographed work, date of completion, your copyright notice (a *c* with a circle around it ©, the year of completion or publication and your name), and an arrow indicating the correct orientation of the original work (arrow should point to the top). A reference number may correlate to an information sheet with further information. On the back, note your name, address, and phone number including area code.

Some of the labor can be taken out of this time-consuming process if you have your name, address, and phone number put on a stamp made specifically to fit the slide mount. Another stamp containing your copyright notice without the year can be made. If your slide mounts are plastic and resist ink, use white self-adhesive labels cut to fit the slides. These are available in discount and stationery stores.

Store and present your slides in *slide sheets*, heavy clear plastic sheets containing up to twenty individual pockets, one slide to each pocket. Most have holes for storage in a three-ring binder or portfolio. If you're mailing or leaving behind only a few slides, cut down the slide sheet to accommodate the number of slides, rather than sending or leaving an entire slide sheet with only four or five slides in it.

Photographs

Photographs as samples can be black and white or color, whichever is most appropriate to your work. The preferred size is 8″ by 10″, although 5″ by 7″ prints are acceptable. They can be used in a portfolio or in a mailing package as returnable or nonreturnable samples. Shots of your work can be made by a professional photographer, or you can do them yourself. Both options are covered later in this chapter.

Photos are light and relatively inexpensive and a special apparatus isn't needed for viewing. Once the work is shot, the photographic print can be enlarged or reduced in size to fit a particular need. From a negative, numerous duplicate prints can be made with less degradation of the image than occurs in slide duplication. There is more latitude in the darkroom to crop the image—to print only the part of the negative that's considered a desirable image, compensating for errors that might have occurred during the photography session. For black-and-white photographs, you can request a contact sheet and review the printed negatives before deciding which you want enlarged and printed. Sequential photographs, those in a series providing a history of the project from thumbnail sketches to finished product, are easily produced to give the art director an indication of your creative thought processes and proof that you can follow a project through from beginning to end.

There are some disadvantages to photographs; they never have quite the visual impact of a projected slide; they require more storage space; and they can become bent and tattered if not cared for properly.

The characteristics of a "good" photograph are essentially the same as with slides, which were discussed on page 39.

When having photographic prints made from your negatives, research the photography lab before agreeing to let them do the work. Ask other artists for lab recommendations; ask what they did and didn't like about the prints they received. Photography store sales personnel sometimes can provide recommendations; ask if the recommendation is based on personal experience. Talk to the lab personnel; explain your need for clarity and accurate color. Get price quotes—labs have cut-off points where prices change and you might be further ahead to get 100 prints rather than the 50 you'd originally estimated *if* you will use them.

Find out prices for contact sheets of black-and-white work. If possible, take an old contact sheet to the lab with you, and have the lab personnel use it for a test run to make sure they understand your instructions and grease-pencil markings.

Cibachrome is a trade name for a positive-to-positive color photographic process, which means that a negative is not involved; rather the photograph is produced directly from your color photograph, transparency, or original work. The quality varies depending on the quality of the piece being copied, whether it's being reduced or enlarged, and the expertise of the person operating the machine. Some graininess and color shift can occur, especially in flesh tones. Glossy- and matte-finish photographs are available. Cibachromes can be considered if you need a fast photograph of a slide or original work to slip into your portfolio, but for numerous copies, you will most likely pay less to have your work photo-

graphed and reproductions made from a negative. Some copying service centers offer Cibachromes.

All photographs should be labeled with the same important information that is placed on slides. (See section on labeling slides earlier on page 41.) Use the back of the photograph for all labeling, but don't write directly on it, because disfiguring marks will come through to the front. Instead, buy white, self-adhesive labels at any discount, drug, or stationery store and type or print your information there.

Two or more labels are often necessary. A time-saving tip: Place a sheet of labels in a typewriter and fill them with your repetitive information, such as your name and address. Putting this information on a rubber stamp further reduces labeling time. Have self-adhesive labels printed with your name, address, and logo for even more convenience, visibility, and unification of your entire marketing "package."

Photographs can be stored in the boxes you receive from the photo lab when you pick them up or in any appropriate-size box that keeps them from sliding and bending. Acetate or vinyl "sleeves" protect photographs in portfolios and mailing packages. Acetate is cheaper, but scratches easily. Both types of sleeves can be purchased with holes to accommodate three-ring or "toothed" binders.

Whether you select photographs or slides as the sample of choice, keep at least one copy in a file in your studio. This personal studio portfolio is invaluable in case there's a call from a previous client who wants an illustration "like the one you did for us before," or from a writer who wants to do a story on you and needs examples of your work to run with it. If you're extremely prolific in your art production, there won't be time to photograph everything, but make an effort

to have the most successful and well-received pieces reproduced.

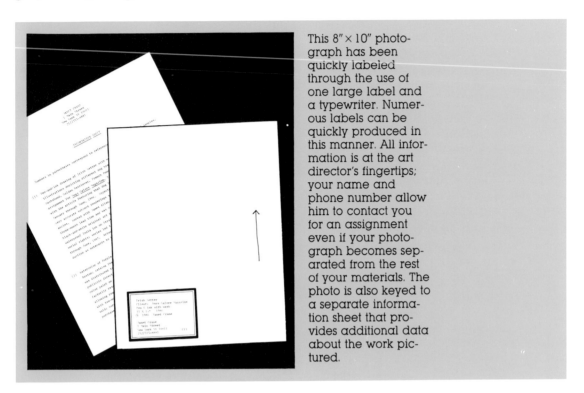

This 8″ × 10″ photograph has been quickly labeled through the use of one large label and a typewriter. Numerous labels can be quickly produced in this manner. All information is at the art director's fingertips; your name and phone number allow him to contact you for an assignment even if your photograph becomes separated from the rest of your materials. The photo is also keyed to a separate information sheet that provides additional data about the work pictured.

Photostats

Photostatting is an inexpensive positive-to-positive photographic process that creates a high-contrast, deep black image on brilliant white paper; it is recommended primarily for black-and-white line work. Photostats are inexpensive and so they make good nonreturnable samples in mailing packages and leave-behinds; they can also be used in portfolios.

In the photostatic process, work can be enlarged or reduced in size. This allows odd-size work to be reproduced on uniformly sized sheets for the portfolio and mailing package.

Corrections can be made on the original work. Type-correction fluid or white tempera are ideal for small

changes, or entire sections of an original piece or a tearsheet can be blocked out with white paper. For example, if you want to use an illustration as a sample, but don't want to include the accompanying printed text or company name, the extraneous material can easily be excluded.

On the minus side, photostats are not usable for color work. They don't offer as "slick" a presentation to prospects as do slides and photographs, and they bend and tear if not protected. Label all photostats, especially those that are to be retained in an art director's file or included in a mailing package. Writing on the back can cause disfiguring marks on the front, so type or print your information on self-adhesive labels.

Include a one- or two-word description or title, name of client (if applicable), medium, size of the photostatted work, year of completion, your copyright notice, an arrow indicating the correct orientation of the original work (arrow should point to the top), and your name, address and phone number including area code. A reference number correlating to an information sheet may be included.

Photostats can be stored in any appropriate-size box that keeps them from sliding and bending. Acetate or clear vinyl "sleeves" protect photostats in portfolios and mailing packages. Acetate is cheaper, but scratch-

es easily. Both types of sleeves can be purchased with holes to accommodate three-ring or "toothed" binders.

Photostatting services are available in most cities and are listed in the Yellow Pages and business directories. Give the operator clear verbal or written instructions so that you obtain the best photostats possible. Solicit opinions about how well your work will reproduce, and make suggested technical alterations whenever feasible. Use the advice also to improve subsequent work; this type of expertise is valuable and helps ensure your getting maximum marketing advantage from your samples.

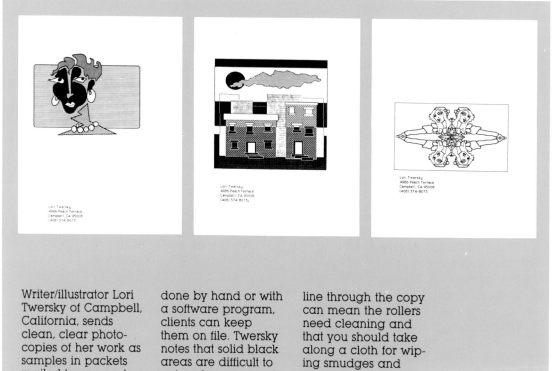

Writer/illustrator Lori Twersky of Campbell, California, sends clean, clear photocopies of her work as samples in packets mailed to prospects. Because of the convenience and low cost of these samples of her b/w illustrations done by hand or with a software program, clients can keep them on file. Twersky notes that solid black areas are difficult to get and recommends Kodak copiers because of the density of their blacks. She cautions that a grey line through the copy can mean the rollers need cleaning and that you should take along a cloth for wiping smudges and dust from the glass. For inperson reviews, she uses originals in her portfolio.

Photocopies

A photocopy is the least expensive of reproductions made by photographic means. Photocopiers are the commonplace machines available in the library, business office, drugstore, or copying center. These machines produce a direct positive image on nonphotographic papers. Photocopies are not recommended for the portfolio, but work as nonreturnable mailed and leave-behind samples.

On the copier, work can be enlarged or reduced, allowing odd-size samples to be reproduced on same-size paper to provide uniformity in the portfolio and mailing packages.

The cost to have the copies made is minimal and numerous reproductions from the original are possible. A variety of papers and lightweight cardboards can be used, since the process isn't restricted to photographic papers.

Photocopiers vary in quality of reproduction. To present a photocopied sample, you must be certain the copies are crisp, clear and clean, free of dots, smudges, extraneous lines.

Photocopies are recommended for black-and-white work only. Color photocopying is available, but the ability to match a wide range of colors is still limited, and "muddy" reproductions can result. Talk with the person operating the machine and ask advice on the quality of reproduction you'll receive for your type of work. Color photocopies are more expensive than black and white.

Some size restrictions apply: many machines cannot handle work larger than 11" by 17". Enlargement and reduction capabilities also vary by machine.

Photocopies don't possess the "snap" that photostats offer and so don't present as professional-looking

a package. They bend, wrinkle, and tear easily.

When choosing a photocopying service, explain your use for these reproductions to the operator and request that special attention be given to the copies. Inquire about paper selection; heavier-stock paper or lightweight cardboard increases the professional appearance of the samples.

Label all photocopies, especially those that are to be retained in an art director's file or included in a mailing package. On white, self-adhesive labels, type or print a brief one- or two-word description or title, name of client (if applicable), medium, size of the photocopied work, year of completion, your copyright notice, an arrow indicating the correct orientation of the original work, your name, address and phone number. You may add a reference number correlating to an extra information sheet.

Photocopies can be stored in any appropriate-size box that keeps them from sliding, wrinkling, and tearing. Acetate or clear vinyl "sleeves" protect photocopies in mailing packages. The cheaper acetate scratches easily. Both types of sleeves can be purchased with holes to accommodate three-ring or "toothed" binders.

Original Work

Original artwork is the most communicative of sample types since it allows the prospective buyer to experience firsthand your style, medium, use of color and medium, and artistic ability. Among its disadvantages: works vary in size and, especially if they've been used for assignments, may include overlays and have printers' instructions in the margins.

Original work must be protected from constant handling. Mounting them on mat board with spray adhesive or rubber cement (or double-stick tape for a less-permanent bond) and framing them with matting not only creates uniformity if all matting is cut to the same size, but also provides something to hold besides the work itself. Placing a sheet of clear mylar between the artwork and the outside matting protects against spills. If a reviewer elbows a cup of coffee over your artwork, the matting is stained, but the artwork should be coffee-free. Matting may also hide old overlay attachments and printer's instructions. If not, redraw the artwork or create pieces specifically for your portfolio. Giving yourself "assignments" for illustrations, comprehensives, layout design—any element you feel is lacking in your portfolio—is an excellent way to round out your presentation while keeping yourself creatively active.

Use original work for in-person reviews, but seldom, if ever, include it in a mailing package. With all the reproduction processes available, there's no reason to risk its loss. There is also a risk of loss when the portfolio is "dropped off" at the office of a potential client and picked up after review. Many artists do include original work and take the risk of its being lost because they want this client to see their best portfolio. In most cases, there is no loss, but it can happen. If you're uncomfortable with leaving original works out of your sight even for a few hours, invest in excellent, suitable reproductions and make them your drop-off portfolio.

The size and number of original pieces dictate the type and size of the portfolio case, since it must be large enough to accommodate your largest original piece. Remember that the potential buyer must be able to handle the matted work comfortably; if it's

larger than 18″ by 24″ the desk may not accommodate it. Have large works reduced and select a smaller piece to present as original work.

If possible, label the backs of all your work with pertinent information or use reference numbers and an information sheet as described earlier.

Tearsheets

Tearsheets show final products of your work. Examples include the magazine page containing your editorial illustration or ad design, the annual report you designed, or the greeting card you illustrated.

Tearsheets demonstrate how your work appears in print, allowing an art director to see and handle an actual piece you created and this adds credibility to your resume.

Tearsheets easily become torn and fingermarked; yellow with age; are difficult to present easily in a portfolio, especially if they are different sizes and types; and can be hard to obtain if your client forgets to supply them. (One way to be more certain you receive tearsheets is to designate in your job agreement that a specific number be given to you.)

If you're presented with the opportunity to select your tearsheets, choose the truest printed examples. The printing was most likely out of your control, and the appearance of your artwork may have been compromised. Problems may include too little or too much ink on single-color art; poor registration or fit of colors or other elements on multiple-color work; smeared or blemished portions of your image. Search for and accept only those that portray as closely as possible the quality of the work you submitted.

Frequently you are left with a single printed copy of your work. To keep this piece clean and intact yet still be able to use it as a sample, you have several options:

- Protect it with a mylar cover in your portfolio and hope the art director doesn't take it out.
- Photograph it as slides or prints and use these as your samples while the original piece stays safely at home.
- Mount it on mat board so that the piece itself can't be handled.
- Laminate it after photographing it.
- Ask the client's permission to have it reprinted at your cost for use as a sample of your work.

If you own multiple tearsheets of the printed piece, you may allow the art director to handle the piece. Replace it with a new tearsheet when it becomes dirty and worn. Use tearsheets as mailed samples only when you have a large quantity or the client's potential warrants them. Tearsheets are difficult to label, especially if the piece is to be viewed on both sides. If only one side contains your work or the tearsheet is mounted on mat board, attach self-adhesive labels containing your pertinent information to the back. If tearsheets are in acetate or vinyl covers or laminated so that the entire piece can be seen, attach a small self-adhesive dot bearing a reference number. Correlate the number to an accompanying information sheet.

DESIGN SAMPLES

Designers have the most difficult job of all in communicating their talent and skills to potential clients. These creative directors want to understand a designer's thought processes, to see more than a finished product. Their main concern is how and why the designer arrived at this solution for the project, concept, budget, and client.

For a first-hand look at the design-portfolio review from an art director's perspective, see page 48.

Design samples must be more comprehensive than illustration samples. So that your samples answer the questions in the creative director's mind, include everything—thumbnails, roughs, final sketches, comprehensives, and finished product—for at least one of your design projects.

If you're preparing a presentation for in-person reviews, your thumbnails, roughs, comprehensives, and the final product must be organized and displayed so that they can easily be reviewed in order. Clear vinyl sheets, heat-sealed on the bottom to form one large pocket, can be cut down to desired sizes so that your materials can be slipped in and out easily. Vinyl sheets with three-ring holes can be placed in a portfolio and turned in proper order. Be sure pockets are clearly identified with self-stick labels or reference numbers.

Another presentation that works well is to cut pieces of mat board the same size and mount your pieces in viewing order, several pieces to each board. In essence you've created a series of storyboards. By presenting them one after the other, you can show your ability to start with a concept and follow through to a finished product. An additional advantage is that your samples don't become torn and smudged from repeated fingering; a drawback is that the client be-

THE DESIGN PORTFOLIO

Doug Diamond is a partner in Diamond Art Studio in New York City, a highly successful art and design studio employing fifty artists and designers. He has reviewed numerous portfolios and knows their strengths and weaknesses. His comments reveal the type of information he seeks when he's reviewing a designer's work.

"When a designer just sends something through the mail like a brochure or an annual report, an art director has a hard time even knowing if he really designed it. Maybe he's worked under someone who *really* designed it or had a very competent production department that did a lot of the design elements for him, such as drawing the lettering or selecting type. These are skills that the designer himself should have, and it's very difficult to determine if he has them by simply looking at a finished piece, even if it's in a portfolio.

"I have to meet with the designer and talk with him and see how he responds.

I'll question him—how did you go about doing this? What did you have in mind? I can get the idea of how he handled the project or could handle it.

"When I review a design portfolio, I like to see the comprehensives and the finished piece. I like to see how a designer works. Any design studio, ad agency or company goes through a process—you don't just tell a client you have what he has in mind and then instantly produce a gorgeous, full color brochure. First you have to go through stages of design, and if a designer can represent those stages with nice, clean, readable, attractive layouts, rather than having to write notes so that the studio can make the layouts, he's much more valuable.

If you're a designer it helps if you can do comprehensives and mechanicals. You should also be able to do your own lettering, to indicate illustration placement, and know typography well. These are all things that are difficult to tell from a portfolio."

comes an observer rather than a "hands-on" participant in the showing.

Once you have presented an entire project that communicates your range of design skills and thought processes, additional final printed products that you've designed can follow in full-size vinyl or acetate sheets.

If you're using the mail to look for a design assignment, have all of the pieces—thumbnails to finished product—photographed, and present your information via a sequential slide or photographic show. An accompanying information sheet is mandatory. Follow your mailing with a personal phone call or, better yet, call before you send your package so that the

creative director can be on the alert for it. Follow up with another phone call within a week.

As Doug Diamond succinctly puts it, "If you want to get contacts, you have to make the contacts personal."

PHOTOGRAPHING YOUR ARTWORK

Hiring a Photographer

Search for a photographer who is experienced in shooting two-dimensional artwork and who understands the importance of this copy of your artwork, even if it means extra time on your part. Ask to see previous photographs or request the names of other artists for whom he or she has worked.

Discuss fees before any shooting begins. Some photographers charge a flat fee, some an hourly fee. Ask if there is an extra charge for developing and printing. In some cases it's less expensive for you to take the undeveloped film to a film lab.

Decide if you want both color and black-and-white photography. Even if you work in color, at times it's advantageous to have black-and-white prints for publication. It's easier for the photographer to shoot everything at one sitting and saves you time and money.

Be sure you own the print negatives. You want the clear understanding (preferably in writing) that you, not the photographer, own the negatives and all rights to the works.

It's also important that you understand the photographer's policy on customer satisfaction before the work begins. If you're dissatisfied with the final product, some will reshoot the works at no cost; others charge half price; still others require full price.

Photographing Your Own Works

Always photograph your work indoors to ensure complete control of the lighting.

You'll need the following equipment to do your own photography:

- A 35mm single lens reflex (SLR) camera with a lens. The most common lens size is about 50mm, depending on the brand. To photograph small pieces, you must be able to get the camera close enough to fill the entire frame with the piece in sharp focus. A macro lens or a close-up attachment gives you this capability.
- A cable release.

- A sturdy tripod.
- Film.
- Two floodlights.
- Floodlight reflectors and stands.
- A Kodak Gray Card.
- Neutral sweeps or background.
- A diffusion screen or photographic umbrella for each floodlight to control reflections if the work you're photographing is glossy.

Owning all of your equipment requires a substantial investment. If you photograph your work consistently, the investment will be worthwhile in the long run. A friend who is knowledgeable about camera equipment may help you check out used equipment through either a reputable camera store or photography magazines (*Popular Photography*, *Modern Photography*, for example). Secondhand equipment is much less expensive than new. If you're merely experimenting with photography, investigate renting or borrowing cameras and accessories.

The film you use depends on the type of sample you want. For color slides, use Kodak Ektachrome Tungsten with an ISO of 50; for color prints, use Kodacolor VR-G with an ISO of 100; and for black-and-white prints, choose Plus-X with an ISO of 125.

Buy two 3200-degree Kelvin bulbs for your floodlights; if you're using Kodacolor VR-G, you also need an 80A color compensating filter with this light source. Check with the photography store personnel for other options and best combination of film, filters, and floodlights for your specific needs.

Hang your neutral background against a blank wall. Attach the piece you're photographing to the back-

Chicago artist Dave Krainik uses a four-color 8½" × 10¾" flyer to promote his pen-and-ink with colored pencil illustrations and caricatures. A realistically rendered corkboard background supports samples of his work. Printed on lightweight coated white stock, the piece is ideal for inclusion in a packet mailed to prospects, or left behind after an inperson review. The mini-poster quality of Krainik's flyer lends itself to hanging in an art buyer's office.

ground with a low-tack adhesive (available in graphic-art supply stores). Secure your camera to a tripod and attach the cable release so that you can trip the shutter without shaking the camera. Check the camera for height and alignment parallel to the work. Move the camera until the piece fills the frame in sharp focus.

Arrange the floodlights, one on each side, at 45 degree angles to the piece until flat, even illumination is achieved. One way to check for even illumination is to hold a piece of white paper against the piece being photographed. A pencil held in front of the paper will cast shadows of equal density if your lighting is even. Uneven illumination causes one side of the piece to be darker than the other; adjust the lights to avoid this problem.

Use the Kodak Gray Card to determine the correct exposure; taking a light-meter reading directly from the artwork can result in an inaccurate exposure. Place the card in front of the piece to be photographed. Set the f/stop to f/8 and determine the proper shutter speed, 1/15, 1/30, 1/60 of a second, for example. Be sure you have the correct ISO set on your camera for the type of film you are using. Set this shutter speed on your camera. Recheck your focus and alignment, and take the picture using your cable release.

For insurance, repeat the process at the same shutter speed, but "bracket" your exposures. This means taking one picture one f/stop above and one f/stop below your original setting. In this case, you would use f/11 and f/5.6 for the next two exposures. *Record your shots in a notebook.* Repeat this process for each piece. When your slides or prints are returned, they'll be in the order you shot them. You'll be able to refer to your notebook and learn which setting provides the best reproduction of your work.

DEVELOPING YOUR PORTFOLIO

Generically, a portfolio is simply a case for your samples. Portfolios come in all sizes and levels of quality—as simple as a three-ring notebook; as expensive as a custom-made, handcrafted leather binder. The most common portfolio is the black vinyl case, zippered on three sides, with or without handles. The 8½″ by 11″ size is the most convenient to carry, but the least acceptable if your original artwork is slightly larger and you don't want to have it all reproduced. Consider, then, the 11″ by 14″ size, which is large enough to accommodate much original artwork, yet small enough to be manageable on top of a client's desk. Portfolios larger than 11″ by 14″ tend to be awkward for desktop viewing when opened. The larger cases can be considered if you anticipate placing your portfolio on the floor and handing artwork or storyboards one by one to the potential customer.

Most "standard" cases have pockets for loose pieces or leave-behinds; they are available in three-ring or toothed (twenty-eight-ring) binder styles or with no binder spine. When selecting a case, consider your finances, the size of works to be placed in it, professional appearance, and intended use. (Some free-lancers work entirely by mail and seldom if ever present a portfolio. A portfolio that is only for your personal use may be less expensive than one to be presented to a potential client.)

A portfolio case becomes *your* portfolio once it holds your samples. As the chief communicator for you and your artwork, it should present fifteen to twenty of your very best pieces. If the portfolio does its job,

the person who reviews it will remember the outstanding pieces; know when, why, how, and for whom they were created, and see the range of your talent.

Always direct the portfolio to the interests and needs of the client you're approaching. If your goal is an assignment with an ad agency, don't fill it with greeting-card samples—and vice versa. A portfolio isn't static; edit it before each showing. Market-researching the fields and prospects which interest you will fine-tune your choice of appropriate samples for each presentation. How to conduct this research will be covered in Chapter 5.

Works can be grouped according to subject matter (children, sports, automobiles) or by materials used (pen-and-ink drawings, watercolors, marker drawings).

If you're a beginning artist, school work can be placed in the portfolio. But be very selective: include pieces that received special praise from an instructor, were chosen for a school exhibit, or won an award. And be sure this work also pertains to your chosen market area. If not, don't show it; you'll only confuse the client.

If you have no formal art training, believe your school work is not what you want to present, or feel your samples are outdated, work up several projects *as if* you were doing them for a client. Present yourself with an assignment just as an art director would, and carry it out. You have an advantage here: you can assign yourself projects that fit the services you can best deliver while developing a professional-appearing portfolio.

PRINTED MARKETING TOOLS

These materials function as companions to your samples. They sharpen your marketing advantage by keeping your work in front of clients' eyes, providing background information and letting them know your skills and assignment desires. Each fills a particular role, either alone or in conjunction with other pieces.

As you read through these descriptions, keep in mind that, while you need not develop all these materials at once, establishing design continuity at the outset ultimately results in an entire package that's visually united.

If you plan to use a logo, now is the time to design it and like it. It can be a typographic device or illustration created especially for your stationery or an actual example of your work that encompasses the style and subject for which you're best known or which you want to promote. Carry this logo throughout your promotional tools—consistency of image will make you more readily recognizable to buyers.

Brochure

A brochure is a pamphlet, booklet, or multifold printed piece; it usually presents numerous examples of your illustration or design work along with background information; it may also include a personal statement. Its contents may apply to only one market area, narrowing its usage; if it provides a general overview of your range of skills, it is often used with other, more focused pieces to approach specific markets.

Several promotional advantages are offered by a brochure:

- The amount of space provided gives you the freedom to create the very best image of yourself and your work.
- It supplies a great deal of information to a prospect in a single submission.
- It can be utilized for in-person and mailed submissions.
- It can stand by itself or work in conjunction with other materials.
- It can be a self-mailer.

A brochure's greatest disadvantage is cost. The same space that allows you the freedom to include numerous examples also incurs a high printing and paper expense. Reduce your brochure's cost with black-and-white reproduction rather than full color; have firm goals for the brochure in mind so no dollars are wasted; and plan your design to coordinate visually with your other materials to contribute consistency of image and name recognition.

The design is limited only by your imagination but, because a brochure can fill a multitude of purposes, think through its intended uses before you begin. Some brochures take the place of resumes by outlining your education, professional affiliations, previous clients, and awards; others communicate only a variety of work.

Basic considerations for designing a brochure are:

- It must fit in an 8½″ by 11″ file drawer.
- It must contain *at least* one example of your work, preferably more.
- A photograph or self-portrait personalizes your message and gives the potential buyer a special visual reference, since no two people look alike.
- Do not include prices.
- The paper must be heavy enough to sustain rough handling if it

will be used as a self-mailer (one folded side is blank; the brochure is stapled closed, addressed, stamped and mailed without an envelope).

■ Base your design and folding plan on standard paper sizes to save money at the printer.

■ Be sure your name and *at least* your phone number are included.

■ Optional information includes brief project descriptions corresponding to pictured works, original artwork sizes and media, and brief quotes from people of influence in your particular field (if they've really said them) or from articles written about you.

If most of your work is color but you are reproducing your brochure in black and white, select works that hold up best compositionally without color to rely on. An option: consider two-color printing, which will fall financially between black and white and full-color; your artworks are still in black and white, but touches or bands of color prevent the brochure from looking drab. Printing in colored ink on colored stock presents a one-color-cost way to obtain a two-color effect. Be sure to consider how the colors will affect one another—don't let form overpower content.

After you've designed your brochure, placed your artwork, and written your text, walk away from it. Let it sit for a while and then come back to it. Look at it as if you were seeing it for the first time as a potential client and honestly evaluate what it's communicating to you.

Letterhead and Envelope

Letterhead is stationery imprinted with your name, address, phone number and possibly your logo and a brief descriptive phrase that defines you or your work. At first thought, letterhead might seem to you the least of your worries, but think again. In mailed submissions, your letterhead is the first "art" item the art director sees. This same letterhead can serve for your resume, invoices, cover letters, and assignment agreements.

Select quality paper. Not only does heavier paper feel richer, but you'll appreciate it if written information doesn't show through its matching mailing envelope as it does with less expensive paper.

Better papers frequently have to be special-ordered, especially if you are using a quick-printer. It may be necessary to buy a minimum of 500 sheets. Although this may seem like more stationery than you could ever use, remember that the price per individual printed sheet decreases as the number of sheets increases.

Also, if you purchase enough paper stock for subsequent runs, you will be sure of consistent color and texture. Don't have your entire paper order printed as letterhead because you will need blank sheets for correspondence that exceeds one page.

In designing your letterhead, select a typeface that is *readable*. If your name and address are difficult to decipher, busy prospects won't take the time. Go through the printer's typeface sample book and decide which typeface visually communicates what you want to say about yourself. Here, as in all promotional materials, your goal is to communicate who you are as a professional. Generally speaking, serif typefaces are more traditional and readable, while sans serif typefaces are more contemporary and utilitarian. Script typefaces are fussy

Presenting a consistent image and a unified package was most important to Ferndale, Michigan, graphic and fine artist Jean Casey when she designed her marketing and promotional tools. The striping and typography shown here on her letterhead and business card carry through envelopes, resume and brochure. Casey markets locally and nationally to greeting card companies as well as magazines and children's textbook publishers.

and may be nearly unreadable if filled with flourishes. Some typefaces that look terrific when large lose their effectiveness when printed in a point size appropriate for stationery.

Tips to remember when planning your letterhead:

- Your name and any descriptive phrase, such as illustrator or designer, are placed at the top of the letterhead to promote immediate identification.
- Your address and phone number can be positioned at the top or the bottom—the choice is yours. Include the area code in your phone number.
- When selecting your descriptive phrase use definitive words, such as *wildlife illustrator* or *book designer. Graphic artist* or simply *artist* really doesn't say much to someone who isn't familiar with you or your work.
- White, beige or pale gray are the

stationery colors of choice, but other pale shades are acceptable. Do not choose dark or garish colors; in the business world they connote insecurity and unprofessionalism, and they also make it difficult to read typed correspondence.

- If you're using colored ink for your letterhead, the ink's color combined with the paper's color also has a readability factor. Black on yellow (pale, please) is the most legible color combination, followed by green, red or black on white.

Your correspondence envelopes (#10 business size, $9\frac{1}{2}''$ by $4\frac{1}{8}''$) should match your letterhead. Your name, address, and logo (if any) should be printed in the same typestyle and ink as the rest of your stationery. Large ($9''$ by $12''$) envelopes for mailed submissions to potential clients as well as any other size envelope you believe you will utilize in your business mailings can also be imprinted to match the letterhead if your finances allow.

Business Card

These 2″ by 3½″ cards are familiar to everyone and are invaluable for getting your name around to potential

SMALL BUT EFFECTIVE

Patie Kay uses her business card as a strong marketing and promotional tool and designed it with those goals in mind.

"One of the reasons people remember my business card is that it's extremely simple. It's printed in black and white on a nice quality linen stock. It has a small picture of a white unicorn on a black background; the other half of the card is white and in black printing states my name, "freelance artist," the types of work I do, and my phone number. It's almost like a mini-brochure in the sense that it states who I am and what I do and gives a small sample of my artwork. The client remembers the unicorn.

"I post it in a number of places—printers, art-supply stores—any professional, art-connected business. Because it's black and white and very dominant, it stands out from most of the colored cards, almost like an exclamation point. I post my card high, eye-level at about five feet, nine inches, because most people looking at a bulletin board start at the top. That's where you'll find my card—at the top."

clients. Even the most casual social setting creates an opportunity to present a new acquaintance with this brief communication about you and your work. Cards also provide a means to attach your address and phone number to other promotional materials that don't have them.

Because of the frequency with which your business card represents you, design it with the same care and thought you gave your letterhead. Use the typeface and logo from your stationery if possible. Be descriptive of exactly the type of work you do. For example, if your letterhead contains the description *Illustrator*, continue the description on your business card by adding *specializing in magazine illustration* or *specializing in pen and ink*. However, if you aren't comfortable promoting yourself so narrowly, don't feel obligated to add this information.

Choose from the same colors as for letterhead—white, beige, and pale gray. The typeface you select will be very small on these cards, so ask to see some samples to be sure the printing remains readable.

Resume

A resume is a historical document that summarizes your art-related background. Two types of resumes can be utilized: chronological and functional.

A *chronological resume* is a history of your accomplishments listed in chronological order, either from the present day backwards (called reverse chronological order) or from early years to the present. Reverse chronological order allows a busy art director to see at a glance your most recent clients and accomplishments.

Group your information in categories, each with a self-explanatory

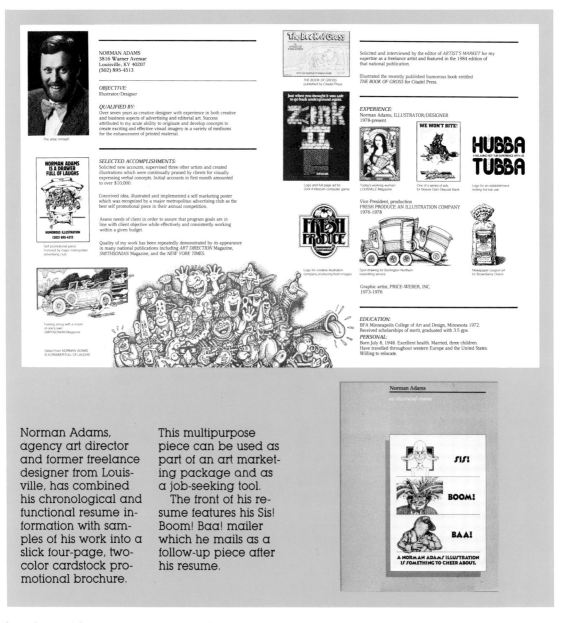

Norman Adams, agency art director and former freelance designer from Louisville, has combined his chronological and functional resume information with samples of his work into a slick four-page, two-color cardstock promotional brochure.

This multipurpose piece can be used as part of an art marketing package and as a job-seeking tool.

The front of his resume features his Sis! Boom! Baa! mailer which he mails as a follow-up piece after his resume.

heading. The categories you choose for your resume should be a factual representation of your background pertinent to the market area you're approaching. If you have more than twenty entries under one heading, divide it into subcategories to be more readable. If you have fewer than three listings, integrate them into a broader category.

Begin with your work background, usually a list of clients that reveals the depth of your experience. If your experience is extensive and varied, break this category into specific market areas—ad agencies, magazines, art/design studios, and so on—with all remaining under the broad heading of *Other Clients*. List first the market area you think of greatest in-

Cincinnati commercial and fine artist Judy Anderson selected a double-size foldover style for her fine arts business card so that she could show samples of her unique pen and ink work. Including samples and all of her business information on a standard-size card would have forced too great a reduction of her line art and text-type, so she has spread the information across three faces of the card. She distributes the card at shows in lucite racks and at personal interviews, and uses the front of a card as a label cemented in the lower right corner of the protective sheet placed over finished illustrations. The three oval details and her logotype also appear on her stationery and invoices. For corporate clients interested in less interpretive work, Anderson has a card she says is "more dignified and commercial."

terest to the field you're now approaching. If your experience is less broad, simply outline your work background under the two subcategories of illustration and design. If the extent of your experience doesn't warrant subcategories, list your clients in order under a *Clients* heading. A year date does not have to appear with each client; all clients for a given year can be listed together. The city and state location of each client can be listed if they are scattered nationwide. If all your clients are in your own city, don't waste space with needless repetition.

If you have held a paid employee position relevant to the purpose of this resume, divide your work experience into two categories, *Employee Experience* and *Free-lance Experience.*

After work experience, decide what is next in importance in conveying your art-related background and professionalism—such other categories as professional affiliations, awards, collections, education, publications, exhibitions. Personal history—outside interests, marital status, health status—may be added last but is completely optional. Most potential buyers could not care less if you're married and enjoy soccer.

A chronological resume must be concise. One-sentence descriptions at most should accompany each listing; within the space limitations of a resume, lengthy written explanations mean other pertinent information is dropped.

A *functional resume* uses brief paragraphs to summarize an artist's ability in specific areas rather than to list items in a specific order. This type of resume is ideal for the new graphic artist or the graphic artist who is changing careers: neither has recent relevant experience.

The same types of headings, such as work experience, illustration, design, and education, are used. However, written paragraphs draw in *all* experience related to the topic of the heading, whether the experience was from life, a volunteer situation, a paid assignment, or part of your schooling. For example, if one of your category headings is *Magazine Illustration*, write a paragraph about your experience and responsibilities as art director for your school bulletin, the illustrations you did as a volunteer for the local National Association of Retired Persons, the two magazine illustration assignments you fulfilled, the summer job you held at a printer's and, most important, what you learned about illustration through these experiences and how this knowledge will help the client you're now approaching. You can also include travel and hobby experiences *if* they legitimately relate to and enhance your art experience.

Keep your paragraphs short and the language descriptive. You can include a statement about your goals or an art analysis if you desire, but don't crowd out more important information. If you don't have any formal art education, list workshops and seminars you've attended and any well-known person under whom you may have studied. Head this category *Art-related Education.*

Be honest, but use these paragraphs to pull in every aspect of your life that has influenced your graphic arts career and made you the talented and resourceful person you are today.

Any resume should be one page, definitely no more than two. Always begin with your name, address, and phone number including area code. Make your resume visually attractive and readable through the creative use of underlining, boldface type, capital letters, indenting, and bullets. Be consistent; if you use boldface type for one category heading, use it for all similar headings.

A resume is not a static document. You can set up categories in any professional-sounding manner that shows you to your best advantage. Utilize any market research you've done to key your information to your market area.

Organizing information for a resume is often the hardest task of preparing one. Regardless of whether you're looking at an outdated resume or starting from scratch, begin your organizational efforts by writing, in no particular order, a list of all your art-related accomplishments and experience. If you're short on actual job assignments, list accomplishments that can be seen as art-related experience. Write down paid jobs, clients, volunteer assignments, community projects, education, and professional affiliations. Write until nothing more comes to mind.

Review your list and look for categories that naturally evolve from your accomplishments. Search for a common thread. Begin with the broadest categories, such as *Clients, Illustration, Freelance Assignments, Education.* Group your accomplishments under these broad topics and divide them further if your list is lengthy.

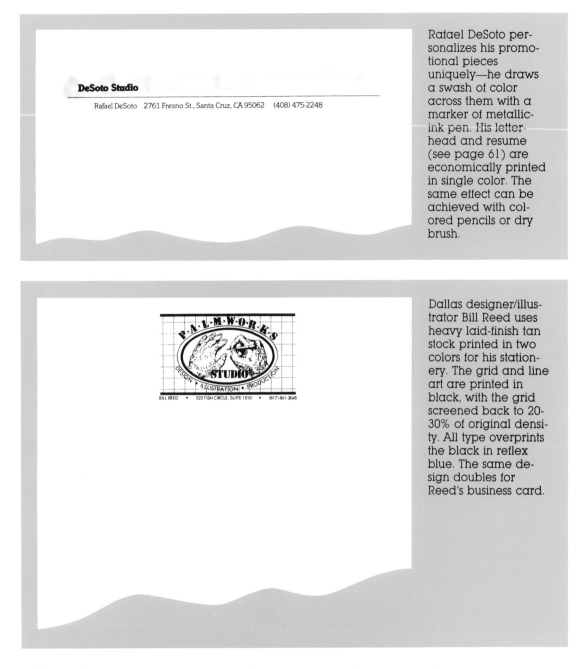

Rafael DeSoto personalizes his promotional pieces uniquely—he draws a swash of color across them with a marker of metallic-ink pen. His letterhead and resume (see page 61) are economically printed in single color. The same effect can be achieved with colored pencils or dry brush.

Dallas designer/illustrator Bill Reed uses heavy laid-finish tan stock printed in two colors for his stationery. The grid and line art are printed in black, with the grid screened back to 20-30% of original density. All type overprints the black in reflex blue. The same design doubles for Reed's business card.

If you discover your resume is four pages long and growing, it's time to edit. Everything is important to you, but not to the client you're approaching. Delete either the oldest information or the least relevant to this market area until you've pared your resume down to one to two pages. Consider deleting even your education entry if it's taking room from information that makes you more interesting and salable.

Don't throw away your accomplishments list. Once you're comfortable

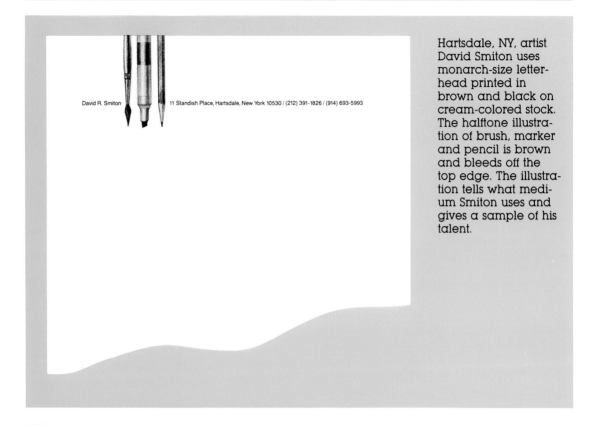

Hartsdale, NY, artist David Smiton uses monarch-size letterhead printed in brown and black on cream-colored stock. The halftone illustration of brush, marker and pencil is brown and bleeds off the top edge. The illustration tells what medium Smiton uses and gives a sample of his talent.

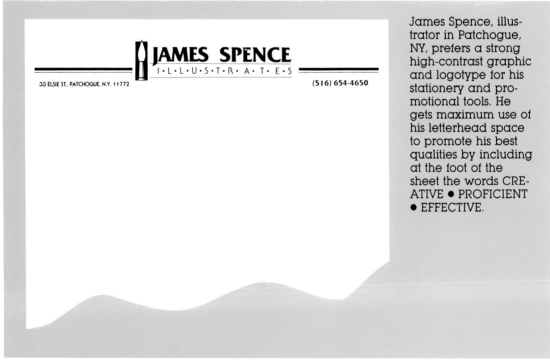

James Spence, illustrator in Patchogue, NY, prefers a strong high-contrast graphic and logotype for his stationery and promotional tools. He gets maximum use of his letterhead space to promote his best qualities by including at the foot of the sheet the words CREATIVE ● PROFICIENT ● EFFECTIVE.

Jean Casey
artist

656 W. Woodland
Ferndale, MI 48220
(313) 398-1962

EDUCATION	M.F.A., Pratt Institute, Brooklyn, NY, June, 1966.
	B.F.A., Washington University, St. Louis, MO, June, 1964.
EMPLOYMENT	Lyceum Computers, Inc., Warren, MI, 1980 - Present. Advertising coordinator, design and illustration.
	Macomb Community College, Warren, MI, 1967 - 1975. Instructor in drawing, painting and design.
	Wayne State University, Detroit, MI 1968 - 1972. Part-time instructor in drawing.
	Hoskinson and Rohloff Studios, Chicago, IL, Summers, 1960,1961. Fashion illustrator.
ILLUSTRATION (free lance)	The NewsLetter, Lyceum Computers, Inc., Warren, MI, 1983 - Present. Illustration and layout design.
	The Friendly Society, New Braintree, MA, 1980 - 1981. Illustration and greeting card designs.
	Birmingham Unitarian Church, Bloomfield Hills, MI, 1980 - 1981. Poster, invitation and place card designs.
	Drayton Avenue Cooperative Nursery, Ferndale, MI. 1977 - 1979, 1981 - 1983. Bulletin board design and illustrations. Logo design.
	Ancona School, Chicago, IL, 1977. Poster and brochure design.
	The Reflector, Macomb County Community College, Warren, MI, 1970 - 1971. Illustrations.
	The Lancer, Washington University, St. Louis, MO, 1963 - 1964. Illustrations.
EXHIBITIONS	Group Show, Michigan Fine Arts Competition, Birmingham Bloomfield Art Association, Birmingham, MI, April and May 1985.
	Group Show, Michigan Annual, Mount Clemens Art Association, Mt. Clemens, MI, March 1985.
	One-Person Show, Young and Rubicam International, Detroit, MI, June 1976.
	One-Person Show, University of Windsor, Windsor, ON, October 1984.
	Group Show, "Animals in Art", Klein-Vogel Gallery, Royal Oak, MI, Summer 1973.
	One-Person Show, J. Walter Thompson Co., Detroit, MI, July 1973.
	Michigan Artist Show, 58th Annual Exhibition, The Detroit Institute of Art, Detroit, MI, February 1971
	Opening Show and Common Ground Show, The Artists Market Gallery, Detroit, MI, May and September 1969.

DeSoto Studio

Rafael DeSoto
2761 Fresno St., Santa Cruz, CA 95062
(408) 475-2248

ART DIRECTOR

OCEAN SPORTS INTERNATIONAL Quarterly color magazine, Watsonville, CA.
GOOD TIMES Weekly news & entertainment magazine, Santa Cruz, CA.
LOUDEN NELSON ACTIVITY GUIDE Community center monthly paper, Santa Cruz, CA.
FOCUS DESIGN & CONSULTATION Ad agency, Santa Cruz, CA.
EMPIRE SCIENTIFIC CORP. In-house agency, Garden City, New York.

CLIENTS

City of Santa Cruz, Parks & Recreation Dept.
University of California at Santa Cruz, Performing Arts Dept.
Santa Cruz Film Council. Annual Film Festival.
Kuumbwa Jazz Center, Santa Cruz, CA.
The Advertising Co., Santa Cruz, CA.
MacMillan & Co., Mineola, N.Y.

SPECIAL PROJECTS

"Artist-In-Residence," California Arts Council Grant (CAC).
"Observations with a Pedestrian Beat," CAC Commission.
"Body Suite, Sweet Body," CAC Multi-Media grant.
Radio Programmer, KUSP FM, Santa Cruz, CA.
Camera Operator, KRUZ Television, Santa Cruz, CA

EXHIBITS (Partial List)

Avery Fisher Hall Corkroom Gallery, Lincoln Center, N.Y.C.
Ponce Museum of Art, Ponce, Puerto Rico .
Institute of Culture, San Juan, Puerto Rico
Bishop Museum, Bradenton, Fla.
Parrish Art Museum, Southampton, N.Y.
Gracie Square Invitational, N.Y.C.
Santa Cruz Art Center, CA.

EDUCATION

A.A.S. Degree in Advertising Art & Design; State University of N.Y. at Farmingdale
Independent study, Art Students League of New York
Cabrillo College, Aptos, CA.

Jean Casey's chronological resume focuses on her art education, employment, freelance work, and exhibitions. She has one master laser-printed on her letterhead and then photocopies it onto her stationery. Using the letterhead reinforces her visual image and boosts name recognition. For mailing packets and in-person reviews Casey includes with her resume a brochure of black ink illustrations broken into such categories as greeting cards, animals and nature, and children's book illustrations. The brochure, as well as other promotional pieces, carry her logo and striping (see page 54).

Artist Rafael DeSoto of Santa Cruz, CA, has repeated the typeface and treatment of name and address from his letterhead (see page 59) on this functional resume. But he has added the graphic of artist with maul stick working on a large canvas to communicate more about himself. As with his other promotional tools, he had the resume printed in black only and personalizes each one with a hand-drawn slash of color, here done with a metallic-ink marker, giving the impression of more costly two-color printing.

with your market resume, transfer all other data to a personal biographical sheet that you'll keep in your files. As you perform a job or receive an honor, place it on your biographical sheet; when it's time to write a new resume or to slant one to a new market area, pull out the pertinent facts. A new resume may come together in a flash.

If you have a letterhead, use it for your resume. Otherwise use white, beige, or light gray paper. Sometimes artists can get away with flashier colors, but don't allow your resume to distract from your other marketing materials. Have it match your business card and stationery as much as possible to create a unified package.

Your resume does not have to be

Artist/photographer Lane Boldman of Cincinnati developed this business card holder to coordinate with her stationery and to keep her card from being lost in a group of materials. The graphic on the holder is a copyright-free mortice printed in brown ink on linen-finish brown stock. The card in contrast is full-color on white coated cardstock; it is held at two corners in slits Boldman cuts into the holder with an X-Acto knife. She personalizes the card and combines her two art areas—graphics and photography—by handtinting the photos of herself.

professionally typeset and printed, especially if you anticipate changing it frequently. Such a resume gives the most professional appearance, but is the most expensive. You can type the resume on white paper and have it photocopied on your letterhead or matching blank stationery. Use your resume in mailing packages and in packets you leave following in-person interviews.

Flyer

If you think of your brochure as a sixty-second commercial, then your flyer is a thirty-second one. A flyer is a single sheet of paper or lightweight card stock with your most vital information printed on one side. It must be eye-catching, dynamic, and designed for immediate visual impact.

To convey your art style, a flyer must show at least one example of

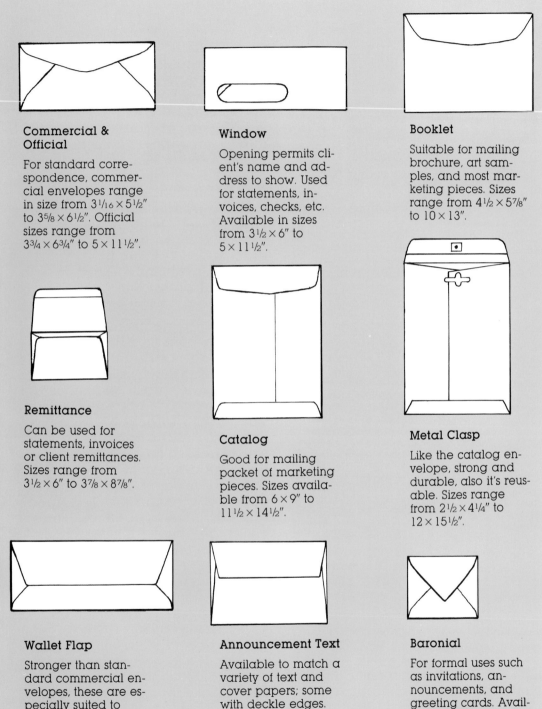

Commercial & Official

For standard correspondence, commercial envelopes range in size from 3¹/₁₆ × 5¹/₂″ to 3⁵/₈ × 6¹/₂″. Official sizes range from 3³/₄ × 6³/₄″ to 5 × 11¹/₂″.

Window

Opening permits client's name and address to show. Used for statements, invoices, checks, etc. Available in sizes from 3¹/₂ × 6″ to 5 × 11¹/₂″.

Booklet

Suitable for mailing brochure, art samples, and most marketing pieces. Sizes range from 4¹/₂ × 5⁷/₈″ to 10 × 13″.

Remittance

Can be used for statements, invoices or client remittances. Sizes range from 3¹/₂ × 6″ to 3⁷/₈ × 8⁷/₈″.

Catalog

Good for mailing packet of marketing pieces. Sizes available from 6 × 9″ to 11¹/₂ × 14¹/₂″.

Metal Clasp

Like the catalog envelope, strong and durable, also it's reusable. Sizes range from 2¹/₂ × 4¹/₄″ to 12 × 15¹/₂″.

Wallet Flap

Stronger than standard commercial envelopes, these are especially suited to mailing of bulky material. Sizes from 4¹/₈ × 9¹/₂″ to 6 × 12″.

Announcement Text

Available to match a variety of text and cover papers; some with deckle edges. Sizes range from 4³/₈ × 5⁵/₈″ to 6¹/₄ × 9⁵/₈″.

Baronial

For formal uses such as invitations, announcements, and greeting cards. Available in sizes from 3³/₁₆ × 4¹/₄″ to 5 × 6″.

The image of a young Elizabethan piper carries over from illustrator Pat Steiner's letterhead and envelope to her business card (see page 66) and here to her resume, with only the boy's position and activity changing. This consistent visual imagery boosts her name recognition. On the resume the piper toots his horn—her horn, in fact—as a lead-in to the functional grouping of educational and professional experiences. The 8½" × 11" sheet of warm grey stock is printed in black.

your work. Brief written text can communicate a self-promotional message, unify the design, or direct the piece to a specific market, but it's perfectly acceptable to provide only your name, address, and phone number, with the artwork speaking for itself. A flyer is not meant to communicate everything about you and your work; rather it keeps your name and work in front of potential customers' eyes and in their mind. A self-portrait or photograph may also be included.

This multipurpose promotional tool is frequently mailed as a follow-up reminder to previous contacts. It can also be used in a mailing package, handed out to clients, or placed in a leave-behind package.

If your flyer is to be self-mailed, choose heavy, good-quality paper since it must withstand mailing conditions. The flyer can be executed very effectively and inexpensively in black and white.

Mailer

The mailer performs many of the same functions as a flyer but is approximately postcard size or slightly larger and printed on lightweight card stock to withstand mailing. An example of your work appears on one side, with or without your name, address, and phone number; the reverse side is utilized for the addressee's name and address. If your name and address don't appear with your artwork, make certain they appear on this side. As seen in Nancy Johnson's mailers in Chapter 2, work or services that don't translate well to single-image representation can be replaced with humorous illustrations or bold, dynamic graphics to get your name and message remembered.

Depending on your finances, mailers can be printed in black and white or color. If a logo or consistent design element appears on your materials, include it on your mailers to maintain continuity of your artistic identity.

The postcard-type form of the mailer allows for inclusion of a personal

Lane Boldman's functional resume serves double duty as a work-sample piece and as a bio-information sheet. Printed as a halftone in black on lightweight coated stock is a collage of samples of her photography and graphic design. The text is boxed in an area knocked out of the halftone border. The logotype is present on all of her materials. Boldman sends the resume with a promotional card and a business card (see page 62) in response to inquiries from buyers. In retrospect she feels the piece is inconsistent with her other materials—too modern for the antique look she has developed.

message if desired—for example, you may confirm an appointment, announce an award, or simply remind clients that you're still very interested in doing artwork for them. Excellent as follow-up reminder mailings, these promotional tools can also be included in mailing and leave-behind packages and as handouts.

Reply Card

A reply card is enclosed with mailed submissions to encourage a prompt reply from the buyer. An ordinary self-addressed, stamped postcard will do, but you can also design a card coordinated with the rest of your materials.

If you're using a postcard, responses appropriate to your client or market area should be typed on the back so that all the prospect has to do is check off a response, fill in some blanks, and drop the card in the mail. A reply card works especially well when no other materials are to be returned. It increases your chance of receiving feedback that suggests follow-up action.

When composing the reply card, put yourself in the prospect's place and focus the responses as much as possible to her or his field. Although not the responses of choice, be sure to include rejection options. Try the following and add some of your own:

( ) We'd like to see more of your work; contact us for an appointment.
( ) We will keep your samples on file for a possible future assignment.
( ) Your work isn't what we're looking for right now; contact us again in _____ months.
( ) Your style doesn't fit our needs; your samples are being returned.
( ) We aren't interested, but thank you for thinking of us.

Be sure to type blanks at the bottom for the art director's name, company name and the date so you know who the card came from and when it was acted upon.

SASE

Another enclosure that requires postage and self-addressing is your self-addressed, stamped envelope (SASE).

Jean Miller uses a beige linen-finish card heat-printed in black and taupe. The image of the lily against a striped shield of solid tone is used on other printed pieces to boost name/image recognition.

▲

Blue and brown ink on cream-colored stock were chosen by New York illustrator Chris Spollen to promote his Moonlight Press. The same tight graphic appears on his letterhead. The phrases *high-contrast illustration* and *We have gone electric* supply explanatory information and pique the reader's interest. See Spollen's flyers on page 34. The card is printed vertically with the graphic positioned slightly higher than center.

◄ No one seeing Fresno artist Keith Hansen's business card could doubt upon what subject matter his art centers. With words and graphic, Hansen details his concentration on winged nature. The card features type and illustration in reflex blue ink thermographically printed on warm grey linen-finish cardstock.

▲

Elizabeth Dewar's business card is unusual and classy in several ways: she has chosen dark blue linen-finish stock, has had her illustration of the carousel horse reverse-embossed up from the face of the card and then overprinted with metallic silver ink, and has used opaque flat silver ink for her typeset information.

308 W. 4TH STREET / CINCINNATI, OHIO / 45202 / 513-579-1874

▲

Illustrator/designer Carol Strebel of Cincinnati carries her logo, typeface, and boxed-name-and-service design across all of her marketing tools, although she is presently phasing out her first name for a more streamlined identification. She clips the cards to other items in mailed packets and uses them as labels cemented to the cover-sheets of her mechanicals. Referrals from printers she has not dealt with but who have identified her work by the card/label have convinced her to continue using the cards this way.

▲

New York City illustrator Barbara Kelley grabs attention with a self-portrait done in her characteristic style. Both illustration and type are heat-printed with raised lettering in black on white coated cardstock. Kelley says the extra expense of the thermographic process is not prohibitive and she prefers the richer, more prestigious appearance.

▲

Pat Steiner's piper takes a pose to fit the standard dimensions of her business card. Using the figure provides continuity of image and style from one promotional tool to another. The cardstock and ink match her resume and stationery.

This clever b/w flyer by Dennis Noblett of Grand Prairie, TX, promotes his cartoon and illustration style and is an ingenious holder for his two-color business card. The cutout thumb in the final panel and the red in his sweater make his business card jump out from the rest of the piece to draw the prospect's attention to his name and phone number. The self-portrait personalizes the card. Noblett had his flyers commercially printed and then cuts out the thumb with an art knife, saving the large expense of die-cutting. He sends these flyers and cards alone, folded inside a #10 envelope, to book and greeting card publishers.

This is the envelope you must enclose in mailed submissions when you want your samples returned. It isn't a guarantee of their return, but without it you can be guaranteed they won't be returned. No company has the time or money to address envelopes to soliciting artists and attach postage.

One vitally important point to remember regarding the return of samples: *No one is obliged by law to return any unsolicited materials they have received.* Most art buyers do make effort to return the materials an artist has requested, but some do not. Send out your samples with the idea that you hope to get them back but you'll survive if you don't. If losing those samples would be a real set-back, rethink what you're sending. Perhaps you should acquire more duplicates or use a less expensive form of sample. Also, be sure the SASE is large enough to handle the samples you've sent and that sufficient postage is attached.

Information Sheet

An information sheet is a 8½″ by 11″ sheet of paper bearing supplementary information regarding the samples you've submitted. Key numbers on individual samples correspond to matching numbers on the information sheet. Pertinent facts include the overall project that included your artwork, the client, your thinking in creating the artwork, how it was used, and so on. An information

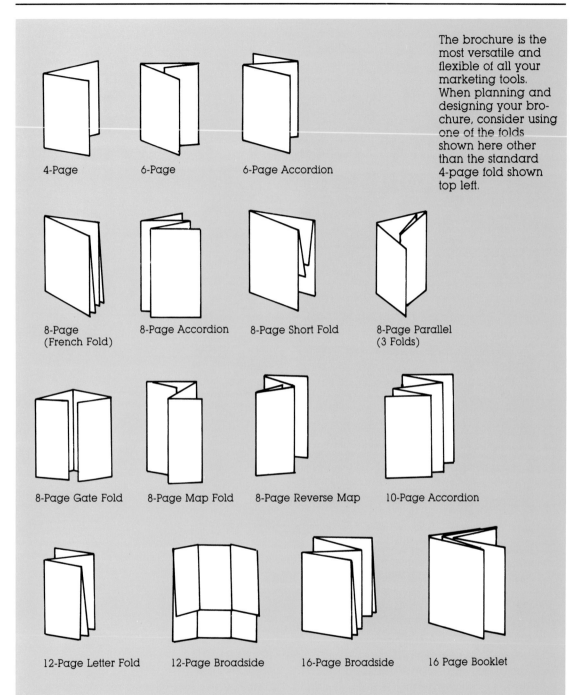

4-Page

6-Page

6-Page Accordion

The brochure is the most versatile and flexible of all your marketing tools. When planning and designing your brochure, consider using one of the folds shown here other than the standard 4-page fold shown top left.

8-Page (French Fold)

8-Page Accordion

8-Page Short Fold

8-Page Parallel (3 Folds)

8-Page Gate Fold

8-Page Map Fold

8-Page Reverse Map

10-Page Accordion

12-Page Letter Fold

12-Page Broadside

16-Page Broadside

16 Page Booklet

Chris Spollen uses two-color flyers for announcements of an address change and a new equipment purchase. Both 10″ × 7″ pieces are printed in brown and green ink on the same buff-colored stock. Pasting up art and copy for both flyers on one mechanical, color separated to make one mostly brown and one mostly green, and having them printed in a single run on 11″ × 17″ stock yields two very dissimilar pieces at a large cost and time savings.

sheet is especially useful with mailed submissions, where you're not present to fill in helpful details.

If your samples are well-established and won't be varying for a while and your finances allow, have your information sheet typeset. However, if the presentation changes regularly, type the information sheet and photocopy it onto your letterhead or blank stationery sheets. Be sure it is readable, uses correct grammar, and is easy to follow.

Leave-Behind

This is one of those items that is exactly what it sounds like—one chosen

James Spence's
5½" × 8½" four-color
mailer is beautifully
printed on coated
cardstock with the
back left blank for
message and ad-
dress. The same
strong typeface and
unique treatment of
his art specialty are
carried over from his
letterhead. The two
main lines of type
are set in weight-var-
iants of the same
family of type.

RICK WATKINS   248 BEECHRIDGE DRIVE, CINCINNATI, OHIO 45216   (513) 281-1234

This 6" × 4¼" mailer
from Cincinnati artist
Rick Watkins is one of
a series of four art-
sample postcard
mailers he had
gang-printed.
Watkins laid out two
screened halftone
and two line art illus-
trations on the same
mechanical, had
them shot and print-
ed on one run in
black on white coat-
ed cardstock, and cut
apart by the printer.
In mailed-submission
packets he includes
one of the series with
a cover letter, a slide
portfolio of his full-
color work, and a
SASE for return of the
slides. The mailer is a
"keeper" for the cli-
ent. Every six to eight
weeks he self-mails
one of the cards as a
reminder to buyers
and prospects.

A standard postcard format, four-color on the front and b/w on the back, serves Lane Boldman's purposes in creating this promotional mailer. Her dual roles as photographer and graphic artist are shown in the handtinted photo; name, address, phone number, and place for personal message are on the back. Boldman sends these in mailing packets, as stand-alone reminders and holiday greetings, and uses them as leave-behinds at personal reviews.

Gary Allen, Samsonville, NY, uses this 8″ × 5½″ b/w mailer to promote his pen and ink illustrations. The fine detail of his work is well reproduced on white coated cardstock. His address and bulk-mail permit on the back leave room for personal reminder messages or holiday greetings. The card can also be included in mailing packages and left behind after a personal review.

BOOM!

☐ Good work—I want to see more!
☐ I'd like to set up an appointment to discuss employment.
☐ We're not hiring but I'd like to discuss freelancing.
☐ (Other) _____

BAA!

☐ Nice, but no cigar.
☐ Take me off your list!
☐ (Other) _____

Please fill out this handy post card and return to Norman Adams.

NAME _____ TITLE _____
COMPANY _____
ADDRESS _____ CITY _____
STATE _____ ZIP _____ PHONE _____

```
( )  We work only with local artists.

( )  We will keep your samples on file and notify you
     if an assignment arises.

( )  Your style doesn't meet our needs.

( )  We're not interested right now; contact us again
     in _____ months.


Name _____  Firm _____  Date _____
```

STAMP

NORMAN ADAMS
3816 Warner Avenue
Louisville, KY 40207

This example of a typed reply card has responses that could be used for ad agency art directors. The wording here was selected to gather information about the firm's policy on working with out-of-town artists. If the firm works only with locals, you may want to eliminate it from your mailing list. Focus your responses as much as possible on the client you're approaching.

Norm Adams created a distinctive and upbeat 4¼″ × 6″ reply card. On the front two-thirds of the self-addressed card, portions of his Sis! Boom! Baa! mailer give a light-hearted air to the serious matter of acceptance/rejection by the prospect. All text is typeset, with boxes provided for checkoff of responses, lines for personal comment, and space for reviewer's name, address, and phone number.

piece or a planned packet of materials that you leave behind after an interview. Its purpose is to be kept on file, so that the client can check your art style, your experience, the type of work you'd like to do, and how you can be reached.

When you are just starting out and have not assembled all your printed materials, or when budget constraints demand, your leave-behind can be as simple as a brochure, a fly-

er, or one labeled sample of your work. If your initial contact with the prospective client was by mail with one or more promotional pieces, leave behind a piece not included in the original mailing, if possible, to avoid duplicating the prospect's file of your work.

A leave-behind can also be *several* of your promotional and marketing pieces that work together as a cohesive unit. It can be a combination of

New York graphic artist Glenn Wolff took the occasion of a new telephone listing to promote his pen and ink illustration style to both current and potential clients. This $6\frac{1}{2}'' \times 8\frac{1}{4}''$ one-color, single-side mailer was sent as a standalone to existing contacts and as part of a packet of samples and marketing pieces to prospective buyers. For economy, one image of this size can be combined with another of the same size on a single mechanical, printed on $8\frac{1}{2}'' \times 14''$ stock, and trimmed apart. To get the image to bleed, as here, without being charged extra for it, have the piece trimmed to a size $\frac{1}{8}''$ shorter than the image on all bleed edges.

a brochure or flyer, resume, business card, a printed sample sheet, or one or more actual samples of your work. Some artists insert these pieces in a standard pocket folder. Others have a folder specially printed to coordinate with the rest of their materials. Clear plastic "pockets" also work well, as do clear acetate sheets held together with a plastic spine; all can be purchased at stationery and art supply stores. Be sure all materials fit the standard $8\frac{1}{2}''$ by $11''$ file drawer.

Invoices
An invoice is a billing for an agreed-upon fee, mailed to a client when the job is completed. Standard invoice

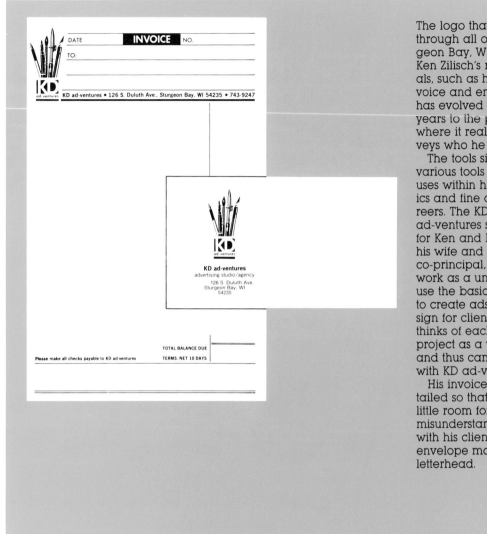

The logo that carries through all of Sturgeon Bay, WI, artist Ken Zilisch's materials, such as his invoice and envelope, has evolved over the years to the point where it really conveys who he is.

The tools signify the various tools that he uses within his graphics and fine art careers. The KD in KD ad-ventures stands for Ken and Diane, his wife and business co-principal, who work as a unit and use the basic shapes to create ads and design for clients. He thinks of each client project as a venture and thus came up with KD ad-ventures.

His invoice is detailed so that there is little room for any misunderstanding with his clients; his envelope matches his letterhead.

forms are available at office supply and stationery stores, but it's better to type the bill on your letterhead or on an invoice form specially designed and printed with your logo, name, address, and telephone number in a style and type to match your letterhead. An invoice that coordinates with your entire package presents another opportunity to give your name visibility and reinforce a visual association with your logo. (See Nancy Johnson's invoice on page 29.) If you're having invoices printed, investigate the cost of carbon-lined or carbonless forms so that you always have a duplicate of the bill. A sample of the carbonless invoice is shown on page 79.

Labels
Self-adhesive labels, imprinted with your name, address, and logo to match your stationery, serve a multi-

Carol Strebel has had such great response to her 35¼″ × 11″ b/w poster, left. The design began as a series of four oil paintings, 18″ × 22″ each, created to hang one above the other. When she designed her marketing materials folder, front and back shown above, she placed the images in a square pattern on the front cover, with her characteristic signage at the top and logo at the foot. She produced the vertical poster after that, showing the four panels stacked. Strebel uses the 8½″ × 11″ folder to enclose a cover letter, printed resume, shown above, 8″ × 10″ color print samples, b/w photostats, and business card. The back of the heavy card-stock folder shows more of her b/w illustrations with a short explanation of their various styles to inform and draw the viewer into closer examination of her work. The packet of materials is used in person and sent through the mail.

Graphic Design
Illustration

NORMAN ADAMS

3816 Warner Avenue
Louisville, KY 40207

502 895-4513

The reverse-out print-ing and the bleed portrait on Norm Ad-ams' business card pull it out from the stack—and economi-cally, too. Adams "played around" with a small photo of him-self, reproducing it on a copier and adding some stippling. He pasted the photocopy and type on a single mechanical which the printer shot as line art and printed in black ink on white coated cardstock.

tude of purposes—and also give your name frequent visibility. Small labels with only your name and address can be used to label the backs of samples as well as the protective coverings of finished artwork or mechanicals. For mailed submissions or shipment of work, use large labels that bear your name, address and logo *and* provide room for the name and address of the recipient. Both accessories increase logo recognition and name identifica-tion and coordinate your entire mar-keting package even further.

WRITING MARKETING COPY THAT SELLS

Brochures have room for the most written text; here the possibility to expand on your qualities is greatest. Don't overdo the written text, but don't overlook this opportunity to blow your own horn, either. When creating written text remember to:

- Brush up on grammar and punc-tuation. Your professional image is dealt a severe blow if misspell-ings and haphazard punctuation appear in your text.
- Use descriptive language. Avoid provoking nausea, but take the time to reread what you've writ-ten and look for sentences where more active or descriptive words can bring them alive. Selectively use a thesaurus to find syno-nyms for lazy verbs, nouns, ad-jectives, and adverbs. For exam-ple, do you consider your work "dramatic"? Then it can also be vivid, expressive, powerful, strik-ing, moving, or touching. Do you "see"? Then you can also envi-sion, visualize, imagine, con-ceive, image, or picture.
- Form sentences that emphasize the words you want noticed.
- Be brief. This text is a selling tool, not a life history. Favor short sentences.
- Organize your information before you begin. Return to the lists containing the good points of your work and your business qualities. Use these as a basis of your text.
- Group similar facts and ideas to-gether.
- Plan your writing so that readers pick up the message immediately and understand it completely.
- Be sure *everything* you write is proofread before it's printed; find a knowledgeable friend or ask if your printer offers this service.
- If you don't feel entirely confident

with your copywriting skills contact a professional writer for help. Perhaps your networking has put you in touch with a writer who would draft your material or edit what you've written for a smaller fee or in return for your art services.

Marketing Tools as Self-Promotion

Your marketing tools, the same ones that sell your work, can also work to sell *you*. To make the most of this dual opportunity, evaluate the message that each of your marketing tools conveys. Be aware that several tools—especially mailers and flyers—

MAKING YOUR TOOLS UNIQUE

You have it all over the rest of the world when it comes to designing your own marketing and promotional pieces—you're an artist, with a highly developed imagination and the creativity and technical savvy to actualize what you envision. So let your creativity fly! Make your pieces unusual, eye-catching, unique. So long as your design doesn't interfere with your message but rather conveys and supports it, you're limited only by your ideas and your budget.

You can make your printed pieces unique in several ways: by what you include, by how they are produced, and by what special touches you add to them.

Including a photograph of yourself or possibly your studio makes the piece distinctive. It will also add to the cost. For economy's sake and because the technique is not overused, don't have the photo converted to a halftone; just paste up a strong, high-contrast black-and-white print—matte or glossy—on your mechanical and have it shot by the printer as one piece of art. This "conversion" drops out all the greys and leaves a dramatic image. Norm Adams' business card is an example of this. Compare that image with the standard halftone printed as part of his resume.

Jean Miller, medical and biological illustrator, provides clients with a photographed sample of her four-color artwork—*with* her name, address, and telephone number a part of that photo. She pastes up both her artwork and the typeset information, which will print below the art in black directly on the mechanical. Instead of taking the camera-ready art to a conventional printer—where the four-color image would first have to be electronically scanned to separate it into yellow, cyan, magenta, and black, converted to negatives and transferred to printing plates, and then recombined on the press into an approximation of the original image—she has the mechanical shot by her photographer and printed in quantities suited to her needs. For small quantities, such as 50 or 100, the cost of the conventional scanning and printing process would be too high for most free-lancers.

Using the same illustration or design element in several ways on different printed pieces makes them unique while boosting name and work recognition. Carol Strebel used four photorealistic paintings, arranged in a square, as the cover of her marketing packet folder. She then rearranged the four panels into a vertical design, as the original canvases are hung, and produced a poster. Both pieces are shown on page 76.

lend themselves to a quick self-promotional message, such as "I meet deadlines!" or "I listen to my clients—it's profitable to work with someone who cares." Your one tool now delivers two messages—one about your work (visual) and one about you (written).

To decide what verbal message you want to pass along, first look into yourself. Make a list of all the qualities you bring to an art business relationship. Flexibility? Diversity? Mechanical skills? Meet deadlines regu-

larly? Work well with people? Humor? Listen well? Know how to be a team member? Conscientious? Take direction constructively? Contribute opinions? Responsible? These are the added elements that broaden your value: an art director needs to be able to rely on creative "team members" to complete projects satisfactorily and on time. You need to inform the client that you're a talented business person who brings more than an illustration or design to clients.

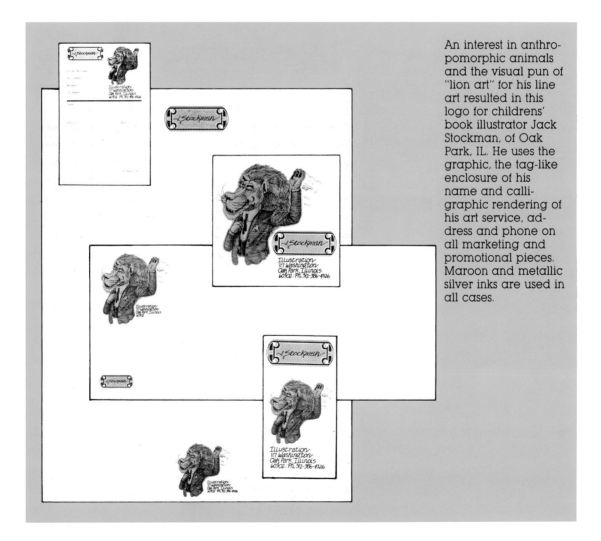

An interest in anthropomorphic animals and the visual pun of "lion art" for his line art resulted in this logo for childrens' book illustrator Jack Stockman, of Oak Park, IL. He uses the graphic, the tag-like enclosure of his name and calligraphic rendering of his art service, address and phone on all marketing and promotional pieces. Maroon and metallic silver inks are used in all cases.

CHAPTER THREE
CHECKLISTS

Marketing Tools

Effective marketing tools are important to your success. The next step is to decide which ones you want to develop:
- [ ] Art samples
- [ ] Brochure
- [ ] Letterhead and envelope
- [ ] Business card
- [ ] Resume
- [ ] Flyer
- [ ] Mailer
- [ ] Reply card
- [ ] Invoice
- [ ] Labels

Quality Slides and Photographs

If you select slides or photos as your art samples, check that the:
- [ ] Color is true and the contrast good for black and white
- [ ] Image fills the frame
- [ ] Background is clean and neutral
- [ ] Edges are straight
- [ ] Focus is sharp
- [ ] Exposure is good and even

Hiring a Photographer

Before you spend a single dime, check that the photographer:
- [ ] Has previous (preferably extensive) experience in shooting two-dimensional work
- [ ] Will discuss fees before shooting work
- [ ] Will establish terms for re-shooting of unacceptable photographs or slides
- [ ] Can shoot type of pictures you desire, color or black and white, slides or photographs
- [ ] Allows artist to own negatives
- [ ] Presents samples of work for inspection
- [ ] Preferably is recommended by other artists

Photographing Your Own Work

You can save money by shooting your own work. To do so you'll need:
- [ ] 35mm SLR camera with 50mm or macro lens
- [ ] Tripod
- [ ] Film
- [ ] Two floodlights
- [ ] Floodlight reflectors and stands
- [ ] Kodak Gray Card
- [ ] Cable release
- [ ] Neutral background material
- [ ] Diffusion screen or umbrella for each light

Brochure

Your brochure should satisfy the following requirements:
- [ ] Is a pamphlet, booklet or multifold printed space
- [ ] Contains large amount of space for work samples and written text
- [ ] Contains at least one art example
- [ ] Stands by itself or works with other pieces
- [ ] Is self-mailable
- [ ] Is your highest financial investment of printed materials
- [ ] Fits into an $8\frac{1}{2} \times 11$-inch file drawer
- [ ] Designed on standard paper sizes to save money
- [ ] Designed with folding in mind
- [ ] Includes your name and at least your phone number
- [ ] Carries through logo and design from letterhead to unify materials

Letterhead and Envelopes

Your letterhead/envelope design should:
☐ Communicate your name, address, phone number and brief description
☐ Advertise who you are and what you do
☐ Be printed on the best pale shaded paper you can afford
☐ Feature readable typeface
☐ Show your address and phone at top or bottom of page
☐ Feature the same logo and typeface

Business Card

The ideal business card:
☐ Is standard 2 × 3½-inch size for easy filing
☐ Is imprinted with same logo and typeface as letterhead; be sure type remains readable
☐ Is a color that matches letterhead
☐ Includes expanded descriptive phrasing, if desired
☐ Is usable for both business and social contacts
☐ Is attachable to marketing materials to provide address

Resume

Your resume should:
☐ Be a history of your art-related background
☐ Be confined to one page, two at most
☐ Provide information specific to your market area
☐ Be typed or printed on letterhead or same paper stock

☐ Begin with name, address and phone number
☐ Be creatively consistent using underlinings, boldface type, capital letters and indenting
☐ Be concise
☐ Use descriptive language
☐ Be honest
☐ Be updated regularly

Flyer

To maximize your flyer make sure it:
☐ Is a single sheet of paper
☐ Contains your most vital information
☐ Contains at least one art example
☐ Is designed for eye-catching appeal
☐ Includes brief self-promotional message
☐ Is usable in mailing packages, leave-behinds, as follow-up mailer or hand-out
☐ Is printed on heavy enough stock to withstand self-mailing

CHAPTER 4
PULLING IT ALL TOGETHER

So far you've taken steps to focus your target market areas, and you've been presented with a range of marketing tools. Your mind is probably skipping in a million directions: each tool sounds like exactly the one you need; design ideas are crowding your mind; you're debating which tool should be developed first; you want to get the most effective use out of the ones you choose. Clear your mind for a moment. Before you can deal with these issues, you have to know more specifics about your target market areas.

First, ask yourself this important question:

Exactly who are my prospective clients?

MARKET RESEARCH: HOW TO FIND CLIENTS

Settling on one or two target market areas clarifies your marketing picture; the next challenge is to find within those areas specific clients open to your type of work, willing to keep your work on file and to call you when an assignment arises. This challenge is called *market research*.

This process of researching—of learning about a variety of businesses and organizations, and finding names and addresses of appropriate contacts—is time-consuming but vital. Through it, you increase your chance for success by reaching only those firms most open to your type of work; you market your product to the consumers most apt to buy. You channel money, energy, and marketing tools to the areas of greatest potential and reduce the chance for rejection.

Research methods change accord-

ing to the target market you're studying. If you're seeking assignments from firms that specialize in print media, study samples. For example, if your focus is magazines, buy or send for one or two copies of each magazine you're considering (there's usually a charge). Frequent newsstands and libraries to review current issues at no cost. Each art director or editor favors a particular design or look, and you need to understand it. Your work will fit some and not others. You can do this type of research with every print field—books, greeting cards, newspapers, record album covers. Most of us can't afford to buy all of these print samples, but you can scour bookstores, record outlets, greeting card and stationery stores; talk with sales personnel to learn what sells and why. Once you begin to identify specific printed works with their creators, publishers or manufacturers, you're on your way to understanding a company's look.

Service-oriented firms, such as art or design studios, ad agencies, and public relations firms, don't always have a characteristic style because their work varies to suit clients' preferences. For such firms you narrow the market by understanding the types of clients they handle and their areas of specialization. For example, an ad agency that specializes in automotive clients is not going to be interested in whimsical drawings of children and infants, but one whose clients are baby-care-product suppliers will be. An art/design studio whose main clients are soft drink and dog food companies will have little use for illustrations of building construction, but a PR firm whose clients include construction firms will have great use for them.

Some firms will send a client list upon request, and you may get the information you need through a simple phone call to the firm to inquire about the types of clients it serves.

SATISFYING CLIENT NEEDS

Patie Kay works hard to make sure her samples are directed to a client's interests and frequently determines those interests through a phone call to the firm.

"I call up XYZ Agency and talk to the receptionist. I simply say I'm interested in presenting my portfolio to the agency but I'm not exactly sure what type of accounts the agency handles. She'll tell me. Automatically, when I make my appointment with the art director, I've got the type of work he or she is most interested in as samples in my portfolio."

When trying to locate clients, a graphic artist can also dare to be different. Patie Kay had a number of contacts through the agency where she trained, but she also developed a unique way of finding new clients.

"I look in the Help Wanted section of the classified ads, in the section titled *Artists*. If there is someone advertising for a full- or part-time artist with skills that I know I have, I call and convince them to use me on a free-lance basis."

Another way to determine a firm's client areas is to read the Yellow Page ads which often give one- or two-line descriptions of a firm's area of specialization. Yellow Pages nationwide are available in most main libraries.

Resource Directories

Resource directories which list company names, addresses and key personnel in markets such as publishing, advertising and magazines, are available in most library reference sections. Because addresses and personnel change regularly in the business community, don't use one that's over three years old. Not all of the available directories can be described here, but especially useful ones follow. (Addresses for these are printed in the Resources section following Chapter 5.)

For information about ad agencies, try the *Standard Directory of Advertising Agencies*. Published three times a year, it contains data on approximately 4,000 agencies. It lists them by state (geographical index) and alphabetically; each listing includes the agency name, address, and phone number; year founded; annual billing; number of employees; association membership; area of specialization; top management; creative and marketing management; branch offices; and a list of accounts. Mergers, acquisitions, and name changes that have occurred since the last publication of the directory are also noted.

O'Dwyer's Directory of Public Relations Firms is an annual publication currently listing 1,600 national and international PR firms and departments within ad agencies alphabetically arranged. Each listing includes most recent address and phone number, principals and key personnel, branch offices, and a sampling of clients.

For information about art and design studios, *The Design Directory* is published annually. The Graphic and Industrial Design Edition presents information on 1,450 design firms and consultants nationwide. Until 1986 the directory incorporated commercial interior firms, but these are now printed in a separate volume. Arranged geographically by city and state, the book also has an alphabetical index and a list of foreign branches. Listings include name, address, and phone number; founding date; number of full-time employees; principals; design services offered; and a representative client roster.

For book publishers, check *Literary Market Place*. This book contains a wealth of publishing information: U.S. book publishers classified by geographic location, fields of activity, subject matter of books published, imprints, subsidiaries and distributors; book publisher listings containing the company name, address, and phone number, publisher/editor name(s), types of books published, number of books in print, and number of books printed the previous year.

In addition to this information, *LMP* also lists Canadian book publishers, foreign book publishers with U.S. offices, book clubs, associations (literary, book trade, advertising, film, press, radio), services and suppliers (book producers, PR services, ad agencies, typing and word-processing services, artists and art services), direct mail companies, radio and television stations and networks, magazines, and newspapers. There is an alphabetical index at the back of the book.

For businesses, consult the *Thomas Register of American Manufacturers* and the Yellow Pages. The multi-volume *Thomas Register* supplies information on U.S. businesses that manufacture a product or supply a service. Volumes 1 through 12 contain the products and services listed alphabetically by state and city. Volumes 13 and 14 contain company profiles listed alphabetically by name with addresses, telephone numbers,

branch offices, asset ratings, and names of company officials. Brand names and an index are also found in volume 14. Volumes 15 through 21 are files of companies' catalogs bound alphabetically.

The Yellow Pages are invaluable in finding local businesses. Each subscribing business is listed under a heading appropriate to its area of business interest.

For magazines, use *The IMS Directory of Publications* (formerly *Ayer Directory of Publications*) and *Writer's Market*.

The IMS Directory of Publications contains information on U.S. and Canadian publications that are published four times a year or more. These include college publications, newsletters, newspapers, daily periodicals, general circulation magazines, trade and technical publications. They are broken down by state or province and city and are cross-referenced by over 900 alphabetical editorial-interest classifications.

Each listing contains the publication name and address, editor/publisher name(s), frequency of publication, circulation rates, some printing information, and a brief subject-matter description. There is also an alphabetical index by name and location for every publication listed in the directory.

Writer's Market is an annual directory of consumer publications. Listings are divided into forty-six categories according to editorial interest. There are also seventy categories of trade, technical, and professional journals as well as greeting-card publishers. Subject indexes guide the reader to book publishers and subsidy publishers; each listing provides the name, address, and phone number: editor/publisher name(s); and editorial interest including fiction or nonfiction.

For newspapers, check *The IMS Directory of Publications*, described above.

For performing-arts groups, consult the *Music Industry Directory,* which provides information on a variety of services and businesses related to performing arts and music. The names and addresses of symphony orchestras, opera companies, and music festivals are included. Also presented are descriptive listings for service and professional organizations, schools and colleges, competitions, music-book publishers and periodicals, libraries, and foundations as well as names, addresses, and phone numbers for hundreds of music businesses, including record companies.

Also covering record companies are *Songwriter's Market* and *Billboard International Buyer's Guide. Songwriter's Market* is a yearly directory listing music publishers, record companies, record producers, ad agencies, and audiovisual firms. Each record company listing gives you the name, address, and phone number, the type of music the company is interested in, and the number of records produced each year. *Billboard International Buyer's Guide* is an annual produced by the publishers of *Billboard* magazine. As the source book for the music and home entertainment industry, the guide presents data on national and international record and video companies, music and sheet-music publishers, audio and video wholesalers, and manufacturers of consumer accessories. Listings include company name, address, and phone number, principals, branch offices, distributors, supplies and services offered. Also

listed are specific industry services, such as associations and professional organizations and record promotion.

The Encyclopedia of Associations not only supplies names and addresses of potential-client associations (if interest-specific organizations are target markets you're approaching), but also presents you with information on associations that might further your expertise. These might be associations that promote professionalism in the graphic arts field, such as the Graphic Artists Guild or the Association of Medical Illustrators, or ones that can add to your body of knowledge regarding a market area, such as the American Society of Interior Designers or the Advertising Typographers Association. Even if you aren't eligible or interested in actually joining an association, it can yield helpful pamphlets, newsletters, and books.

This multivolume reference work contains comprehensive listings on approximately 20,000 national and geographic organizations. Each entry lists the name, address, and phone number; chief official; founding date; number of members and staff; regional, state, and local groups; description of the organization; computerized services; committees; publications; and more. Organizations are indexed alphabetically by name and by key word (area of interest); there are also geographical and chief executive indexes.

Artist's Market, a yearly directory that lists firms and their free-lance art requirements, is also an excellent reference book for locating potential clients. Divided into fourteen chapters, the book includes listings for ad agencies, audiovisual firms, public-relations firms, book publishers, greeting card firms, magazines, newspapers, record companies, and more. Its listing information includes whom to contact within the firm with your artwork, the type of work the firm is seeking, the types of samples and marketing tools it prefers to receive, and whether it will file or return samples. Professional information is also provided through interviews with artists and art buyers and a business appendix. *Artist's Market* is available in many libraries and bookstores or can be ordered directly from the publisher. Be sure to use a current edition, since firms, addresses and art directors change.

Trade Publications

Read trade publications to keep abreast of trends and to learn the "inside" thinking of your marketing area. For specific markets, check the following: ad agencies, *Advertising Age* and *Adweek*; book publishers, *Publishers Weekly*; businesses, the financial pages and business sections of newspapers and business-oriented magazines, such as *Forbes*, *Fortune*, and *Business Week*; for the retail greeting card trade, *Greetings Magazine*; for magazines and newspapers, *Editor & Publisher*; for performing arts, *Dancemagazine* and *Theatre Communications* as well as any of the numerous music magazines; for record companies, *Billboard* magazine.

Many of these publications can be found on newsstands or in libraries. If they're not available in your area, write to the publisher for subscription information. If you're in close contact with other artists who share your interest, consider splitting the cost of a subscription or networking

the information contained in the publication. Publishers' addresses for the trade publications are supplied in the Resource section following Chapter 5 and can also be found in the *Standard Periodical Index*, a reference book that lists more than 65,000 U.S. and Canadian publications that are issued at least once every two years. Divided into 250 subject areas, the book lists consumer magazines, trade journals, newsletters, government publications, house organs, directories, organizations' publications, and newspapers. Each listing gives the name, address, and phone number; editor/publisher name(s); size; frequency of publication; general editorial interest; cost; and circulation. An alphabetical index of all names is supplied at the back of the book. You can also use this reference book as a resource to find other publications directed to your market interests.

As you study each resource directory and publication, pull out the names, addresses, and telephone numbers of every firm that sounds appropriate to your work goals. If the resource you're using supplies them, also include the name of the person responsible for buying art or design, a brief description of the firm, its clients (if applicable), and the service or product it offers. This is your beginning client list for either in-person or mail contact. As you make contact, you'll be filling out a 3″ by 5″ index card on each firm to keep track of the type of contact you make and the response you get. You'll find more about this in Chapter 5.

If you don't wish to do this much personal research (although it *is* the recommended procedure), or if you want to do a large blanket mailing, you can buy prospect lists from private companies offering mailing list services. These firms frequently are found in the Yellow Pages under the heading *mailing lists*. Contact several for price and list comparisons—some carry lists that are too "generic" for your needs, such as lists of art directors that are not broken down into specific types of firms. Others have a minimum number that you can request, such as 500 or 1,000; this is most likely many more than you need right now, and the price will be high. Choose a mailing list firm carefully so that you know you will receive exactly the types of names you desire and the number that's practical for your finances. Many will send a catalog upon request listing the types of firms their mailing lists cover.

If the list that you generate is lengthy or you've subscribed to a purchased mailing list, check into the practicality of hiring a typing or word-processing service to provide you with these names and addresses typed on self-adhesive labels. You can arrange with these services to have the list reproduced on a regular schedule, but it's *your* responsibility to keep it updated for accuracy.

DEVELOPING YOUR MARKETING TOOLS

With client list in hand, you're ready to begin developing your marketing tools, always keeping in mind the types of clients you've selected, your method of contact, and your finances. You've compiled a list of a manageable number of firms to contact with your work. To determine the types of tools you'll need for these contacts, answer these questions:

- Am I contacting potential clients locally or nationwide?
- Will I contact them in person,

through the mail, or both?
- How much money have I allocated to my marketing and promotion campaign?
- How can I budget my money so that my marketing and promotion campaign is a continuing effort?

Local contacts are most frequently made in person or by telephone followed by an in-person review, and for you this means the production of a portfolio and leave-behind materials. Nationwide contacts are generally made through mailed submissions requiring that you first develop those tools that most clearly and fully communicate who you are and what your work is, because they must function without benefit of your actual physical presence. If *both* methods of contact are utilized, you need to develop a portfolio plus printed materials that can do double duty as leave-behinds and as mailed-submission enclosures.

In evaluating your financial resources relative to your marketing tools, first and foremost allocate the most money to the production of the best possible samples appropriate to your work, method of client contact, and market area. Decide which type of sample—slides, photographs, photostats, photocopies, tearsheets or original work—best exhibits your work within the framework of your client-contact method. Three examples follow:

If your work is full-color, your method of contact is in person, and your client area is New York book publishers, be financially prepared to produce a top portfolio of color slides, photographs, or original work and tearsheets.

If your potential clients and artwork are the same as above, but your method of contact is through the mail, you need to allocate sample money originally only to the production of three to five slides or photographs that can easily be mailed; remember you will need as many duplicates as you have planned mailings.

If your artwork is black-and-white illustration and your clients are magazine publishers nationwide, allocate sample money for photographs, photostats, or photocopies for mailed submissions. If your black-and-white illustration is to be reviewed locally by an ad agency, corporation, or medical-complex public-relations director, allocate enough money to accommodate an in-person portfolio review of photographs, photostats, original work, or tearsheets.

The amount of money you *do* spend depends, of course, on how much money you *have* to spend, but it can't be overstressed that you must direct the most money you can to the best samples. By analyzing exactly how you will be contacting your potential clients and investing in the best samples appropriate to your artwork, you'll put your best professional foot forward without overspending needlessly.

Next, determine which printed materials you should develop. The possible combinations of the tools described in Chapter 3 are tremendous so, again, fall back on your method of contact, your type of artwork, and your client area for guidance in determining which tools you need at this point. You'll add to and build on these first pieces until you have a full complement of marketing and self-promotional pieces, but for now we're focusing on what you need to start with on a possibly limited budget. As you create individual printed pieces, evaluate the package they make as a whole. When com-

bined, the package should present the following to the prospective buyer:

■ Excellent examples of your work, with skills, medium, and subject matter directed to his or her par-

Wisconsin cartoonist, writer and graphic artist Chris Roth takes self promotion and marketing seriously and designs his tools to reflect this philosophy. Roth's marketing kit, which includes individual condition of sale and reply forms, and client list, plus three different business cards to reflect the three creative hats he can wear, is modular, designed so that each piece is self-contained. This lets the artist put together a kit to fit the particular client he's approaching. This flexibility also allows him to update and reprint pieces as needed. Roth believes that a marketing kit such as his, gives art buyers the message of professionalism, stability and predictability.

ticular areas of interest.
- Your name, address, and phone number.
- Background information on your art-related career.
- Previous clients (if applicable).
- An indication of the type of assignment you're seeking.

If you're approaching clients in person with your portfolio, ask yourself what you want them to have *on hand* to keep you and your artwork in mind after you leave. A resume, business card, and one or two duplicate samples can fill the bill; or, in place of a resume and duplicate samples, a well-planned brochure with your background information and printed examples of your work. Any one or combination of these materials can work for you; the resume, samples and business card will be less expensive than a full-color brochure. A black-and-white flyer with your name, address, phone number, and a sample of your work may be ideal.

If you're working through mailed submissions, you can use the same combination of materials with your samples, but coordinate the design of your materials and budget your money to include letterhead. The letterhead will be used for your cover letter, can be used for your resume and samples information sheet, and should match your business card. Samples can be returnable or nonreturnable, but if you want them returned be certain that one of your printed pieces contains examples of your work so that the prospective buyer has in hand a constant reminder of your art style and media.

For either type of contact you must also budget for and plan mailers or flyers for follow-up and reminder mailings. Chapter 5 shows you how to set up a marketing plan and calendar; use this calendar to anticipate the costs of an upcoming reminder mailing so you can put money away for it during the "fat" months just in case the mailing falls in what turns out to be a "lean" month. (Free-lancers must deal with the impossibility of determining an absolute monthly income because it fluctuates according to how much work you've done and how prompt the clients are in paying.) Plan the materials for your follow-up mailing simultaneously with your original materials, using the same paper and printing method. *Sometimes* (check with your printer) this larger quantity of printing can save you money. Another option to consider is planning several pieces to be printed together and cut apart later by you. For example, four different flyers printed "four-up" on a single sheet of paper can be separated by you with a mat knife at your studio. The initial expense is greater, but in the long run it's less than the cost of four separate press runs. You can accommodate this larger expense in a month when assets are plentiful and have mailings ready for the months when your budget is tight. Check with your printer for the best and most cost-efficient ways to go in line with his or her press capabilities.

Other points to keep in mind while developing your marketing materials are:

Understand your needs. By evaluating each marketing tool's purpose, analyzing what it can or can't do for you at this point in time, and planning it to work hand-in-hand with other tools, you can put together a strong, visually coordinated package that supplies the information required and promotes a professional image of you as a graphic artist even on a limited budget.

Know the expectations of your market area in regard to the type of presentation it's accustomed to reviewing. Your previous market research should have given you a clear idea of the level of competition you'll be encountering. If you're approaching, in person, large, top-notch ad agencies, your samples must be full-color slides or photographs, tear-sheets or original work, and must comprise a top-of-the-line presentation with money no object. You're up against very tough competition, and these firms' creative directors are busy, quick-decision people accustomed to dealing with professionals who immediately show their best work in only a few minutes. On the other hand, if you're approaching medium-size magazines through the mail for black-and-white editorial illustrations, your samples can be clean, crisp photostats that can easily be viewed at the buyer's convenience.

Focus your materials to your potential clients' interests. Draw on all the information you've gathered about the marketing area as a whole and the specific firms you're approaching. Review and change the samples in your portfolio as you prepare for each interview. Print separate flyers or mailers if the variety of clients warrants it. If you've been tightly selective in compiling your contact list, the same marketing tool may be used for more than one field. For example, if your forte is fantasy art, the same brochure or flyer can be used for fantasy magazines and record album publishers (assuming any written text includes both fields). But if you're hitting gardening magazines

with full-color florals and PR firms with corporate logo designs, develop separate marketing pieces. The two are too diverse to allow a single marketing tool.

Try to develop printed marketing tools that are multipurpose. The letterhead developed for your cover letters can also be used for your resume, invoices, general correspondence (self-promotion—you're constantly letting people know who you are and what you do), and information sheet. The flyer printed on lightweight card stock showing six examples of your work and a client list can be slipped into a mailing package or a leave-behind packet. The paper flyer developed for your leave-behind packet can be sent out as a self-mailed reminder to distant clients.

Realize that no single printed piece will meet all your communication needs on a one-time basis. The brochure comes closest to providing sufficient space to include all the written information you need plus examples of your work. But you can't write a cover letter on a brochure as you can on your letterhead, you can't hand one out at a party as you can your business card, and it's expensive to use a brochure as a notification of a change in phone number. Your printed materials work together as a unit so if finances are limited select several less-expensive pieces to do the brochure's work. As your income increases you can expand your printed materials to include some of the luxuries, such as the full-color brochure, thermal-printed self-adhesive labels, custom-printed folders, and even mini-brochures.

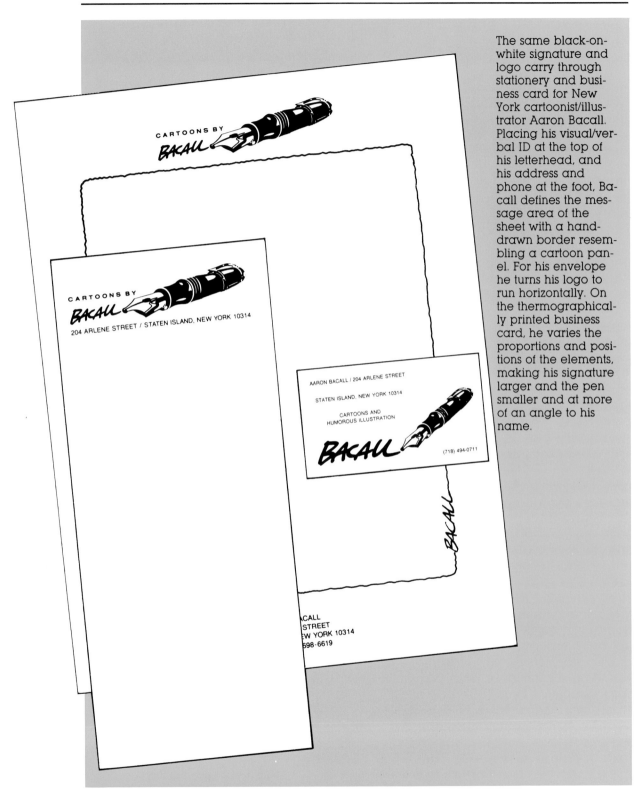

The same black-on-white signature and logo carry through stationery and business card for New York cartoonist/illustrator Aaron Bacall. Placing his visual/verbal ID at the top of his letterhead, and his address and phone at the foot, Bacall defines the message area of the sheet with a hand-drawn border resembling a cartoon panel. For his envelope he turns his logo to run horizontally. On the thermographically printed business card, he varies the proportions and positions of the elements, making his signature larger and the pen smaller and at more of an angle to his name.

CHAPTER FOUR
CHECKLISTS

Market Research

Use this checklist when conducting research into your potential market areas:
- ☐ Study samples of potential clients' works
- ☐ Visit stores that sell you potential market areas' products
- ☐ Talk with sales personnel regarding these products
- ☐ Send for potential clients' client lists
- ☐ Send for potential clients' catalogs
- ☐ Utilize Yellow Pages
- ☐ Research resource directories
- ☐ Read trade publications
- ☐ Fill out index card on each potential client to compile your own client list

Developing Your Marketing Tools

When planning your marketing tools, consider:
- ☐ Scope of client contact, local or national
- ☐ Type of client contact, mail or in person
- ☐ Your budget
- ☐ Type of artwork to be reproduced
- ☐ Each tool's purpose
- ☐ Use of each tool for you at this time
- ☐ How to develop individual pieces to create a visually unified package
- ☐ The needs of your marketing area
- ☐ How to focus all materials to the interests of your clients
- ☐ How to create tools that are multi-purpose
- ☐ Your budget for a continuous marketing campaign, follow-up mailings and updating of tools

CHAPTER 5

THE BUSINESS OF MARKETING

Your first challenge on the business side of marketing is to develop a marketing plan, a series of long- and short-range goals coordinated with a method and schedule for accomplishing them. Your ultimate goal is to be successful in a satisfying career as an artist. The long- and short-range aims keep you on the road to that goal.

With a client list and an idea of which marketing tools to develop, it's time to act.

The creation of art and the marketing of your work and yourself must travel hand in hand throughout your career; ideally, a part of each workday will be devoted to marketing and self-promotion. Realistically, this probably won't happen, especially if the immediacy of an assignment deadline is upon you, but aim for it—what you want to develop now is the *marketing habit*. You want marketing and self-promotion to become as natural and as much a part of your daily routine as is artwork. Plan on spending 40 to 50 percent of your working hours on marketing and self-promotion. If you can schedule the work daily, fine; if not, be sure the time spent is equivalent to two days out of your five-day workweek. Remember that all aspects of marketing and self-promotion are included; driving to the printer, giving a lecture, attending a professional meeting, setting appointments, rematting the works for your portfolio, designing a new flyer—any endeavor and its inherent tasks that you undertake for the long- or short-run purpose of increasing awareness of your work and your status as a graphic artist.

ORGANIZING A MARKETING PLAN

A marketing plan is a series of efforts decided upon because they will help you meet your goals.

Because business is largely carried out on a foundation of appointments and dates assigned for particular operations, you need to develop a habit of thinking along a timeline. Equally important is keeping track of the appointments and the dates you've planned for specific functions. Buy or make a large calendar, a sheet for each month. Large empty squares with a date in the corner for each day are best because you have plenty of space to note meetings and reminders.

At this point many of your short-range goals deal with the mechanics of getting started—selection of artwork to be reproduced as samples, contacting a photographer to shoot your work, getting price quotes from printers, writing copy for your brochure, picking up stationery and business cards from the printer, and so on. Prioritizing these tasks and assigning each to a specific day eliminates procrastination and a haphazard, ineffective marketing program.

Once your material preparation is well organized, it's time to start the actual contact process. It's not necessary to have all of your printed pieces at hand to begin *setting* appointments; just be certain you will have them all by the time you go to see the art buyer.

Setting the interview schedule. If you're going after interviews, assign a day when you make phone calls for appointments. How many appointments you make is up to you; base it

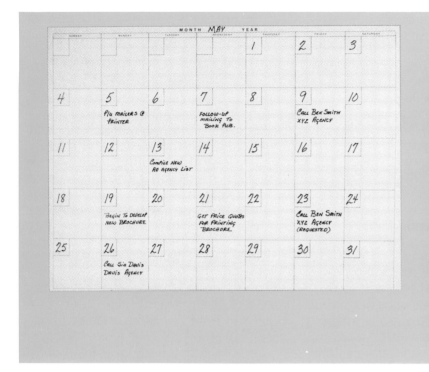

Marketing calendars can be as simple as this one, with the primary consideration to have room in which to write your daily marketing and self-promotional tasks. Although not every block is filled in this example, your calendar should show some marketing effort every day no matter how minor. You must develop the idea that business is as important to your career as is creating your art. The calendar keeps appointments straight, mailings current and your art career organized.

on what you're capable of handling and when you feel freshest. Keep an index card for each contact (or use your computer if you have a suitable program); record the name of the art buyer and firm, address, phone number, date of call, result of call. Also record date information on your calendar: Are you supposed to call back in two days? Mark it in the calendar space two days away—"call Mr. Smith, XYZ Co. to make appt. See index card."

Following each interview, write on the index card the date, results, and your impressions of the meeting and of the buyer's response. A few words will do—just enough to refresh your memory.

It's important to keep your name and work in front of the potential client's eyes as much as possible, so as each interview takes place, assign a day about six weeks away on which you'll do a reminder or follow-up mail-

ing. Using your calendar now to assign the mailing date means six months won't slip by before you remember to do it. Direct this mailing to prospects who have made favorable responses to your work but haven't actually called with assignments.

Reminders can be in the form of flyers or mailers and, depending on your finances, should be sent out every six weeks to three months. Beyond three months, too much time has passed for a mailing to be considered a "reminder." If the time between contacts has been more than three months and you feel this client still has good potential, mail a brochure or new samples rather than simply a flyer or card.

Flyers and mailers used for reminder mailings should *always* contain fresh images. Either they must be updated and reprinted for each mailing to the same client or, if you've had a series of flyers printed all at once, a new image from the series must be mailed each time. Usually three reminder mailings to a client are plenty; if you still have no assignment, decide whether to submit new samples or call for another appointment because this is a client you really want to pursue, or to drop the firm from your mailing list.

Setting the mailed-submission schedule. If you're marketing through mailing packages, gather your materials and assign a day on your marketing calendar when you will collate your packages, pick up your labels from a word processing service or run them on your computer/printer, and mail them. Also at this time, choose a day six weeks to three months in the future for a follow-up mailing, and write it on the calendar.

Compose a master card that describes the samples and printed pieces included in this mailing to avoid accidental repetition in reminders. The master card could read: Package 1: samples—six photostats of pen and ink drawings of horses; brochure of animal drawings; cover letter for editors of animal magazines; business card. On index cards for clients who receive this mailing simply write *Package 1* and you'll know exactly what you sent.

Keep track of the mailing either on index cards or your computer. Record

- The name of the art buyer.
- Firm.
- Address.
- Phone number.
- Date of mailing.

Unless you use reply cards in your package (and perhaps not even then)

Maintain a file of index cards like these. The amount of detail you place on each card is a personal decision, but the more you briefly jot down, the more you'll remember later. Be certain to note a prospect's or client's name, current address and phone number along with your contact method and date.

MARKETING TRICKS

Intending soon to be expanding her marketing from Los Angeles to New York City book publishers, artist Patie Kay is planning her mailing package and shares her marketing expertise:

"Most corporations have a slogan: KISS—Keep It Simple, Stupid. This is what I recommend to any artist who is marketing something. An art director is going to look at your package for a *few moments* and gain an overall impression, so don't send five pounds of materials—he's not going to look at it. I recommend two or three samples that have been reproduced well through photographic means, your cover letter, brochure, and business card.

"Never mail anything so that it arrives on a Monday or Friday. On Mondays art directors are worn out from the weekend and have five thousand things to do. They're not going to look at your package. On Fridays they're gearing up for the weekend and don't want to think about work. Time your mailings to arrive on a Wednesday or Thursday.

"Give the art director eight days to examine your work. If your package arrived on a Wednesday, wait until a week from Thursday to call him on the phone and ask if he received your package. What was his impression? Would he like to be informed of the new things you're doing? Personal contact is important in this business.

"Even though I'm in Los Angeles, when I market my work in New York I intend to follow up by phone. If personal contact works in LA, it's going to work in New York, too. This type of contact is also saying that I think enough of my work and am interested enough in his company that it warrants a phone call.

"It's also to my advantage to talk to the art director. People are helpful if you give them a chance. If the art director is interested in my work, I can ask him if he would like to see more samples and, if so, what type. If he says he's possibly interested, this tells, me my work is okay, but something's missing. At this point I can find out what that something is. If the AD says my work simply isn't appropriate for his firm, I thank him and ask if he can tell me from his expertise in the business of any other company that might be looking for my type of work. The art directors in the field have a pretty good feel for what their competitors are doing, the changes and trends in the field. I make sure all information I receive is recorded on my file card. That's why my follow-up long-distance phone call is worth the money to me."

it's not likely that you'll receive a response from these mailings unless it's an assignment. If you do, however, note the response on the index card. If you use reply cards and they're returned, staple the reply card directly to the index card or transfer its information to your computer. Does the art buyer suggest you make contact again in six months? Mark it on your calendar *now*: *New mailing package to Mr. Jones,* Riders Alive *magazine. See index card.*

Keeping and updating your files. Maintaining your daily calendar and index cards together keeps your marketing efforts organized and efficient. The time spent updating the cards and marking the calendar is saved by giving you a clear head for your art, a mind that's not cluttered with worry about forgetting an appointment or wondering when you did your last mailing. Make your index cards work for you by keeping track of changes within firms, especially addresses and art directors. As your files grow, you'll be sitting there with one of the most up-to-date mailing lists for the industry.

INVEST IN RECORD-KEEPING

Norman Adams remembers what he did in the initial stages of his free-lance career and why he should have maintained the records he began.

"When I first started out I had a list of 500 names, address, and so on, and right next to it a column for the followup I planned, remarks, and so on—it was very detailed. Then the more that I free-lanced, the less I felt I had to keep up these records. What happened was that eventually I had nothing to refer to. I found with the older lists I could go over them and say, hey there's this person and that person—I never would have remembered them without that strict record. As a result, I feel that my first contacts were better; the records helped me to keep everything sorted. Any record keeping system that you're comfortable with is the one to use, but stick to your marketing strategy— your planned schedule of contacts. Even if it fails for three months or a year, keep it up, watch it, record it, look back on it."

Marketing is an ongoing process. Don't do one mailing and then sit and wait. Begin to build another list of potential clients through reading trade magazines, networking, and other research. If all interview possibilities in one field are exhausted, is there another related field open to exploration? Examine new marketing areas that may have been suggested to you when you spoke with art buyers. Consider researching one of the secondary interests you previously selected.

LOCAL SELF-PROMOTION

Local self-promotion is accomplished through mailings, volunteering, organization membership, social contacts, press releases, and staged events.

You are the subject of a self-promotional mailing. Frequently a flyer sent to a range of local businesses, this piece introduces you as a graphic artist available for work in the community. Be sure to include a short explanation of all the services you offer.

Mailings are usually 100-200 pieces and, besides printing and paper costs, you have to figure in postage and the time spent addressing and stuffing. Your finances frequently dictate the extent to which you self-promote through the mail, because results are slower and more difficult to see than those that come from direct marketing. A blanket mailing to local businesses will probably not result in immediate assignments because the specific need for your services does not exist at the time in any company you contact or because the mailing doesn't reach the person or department currently searching for an artist. In many cases, information about you and your skills is spread by word of mouth, and this takes time. Mailings are valid, but don't expect an instant return on your effort.

Volunteering time and talent increases your community visibility. Be willing to do "freebies," to donate your work and talent. Libraries, hospitals and philanthropic organizations frequently need brochures and newsletters, and the people involved with these institutions as board members or within the general membership are very likely the people who can do *you* the most good. They are frequently upwardly mobile and the owners of their own businesses. If you're going to sell your artwork, you have to be with and get to know the people who can afford to buy it.

The organization to which you give your art/design services should pick up the costs of typesetting and printing. Set a specific number of hours for the project to control your expenditure of time. Be sure to request a credit line on the final printed piece—this gives your name visibility and your work publicity.

Talk with local graphic artists. This is networking, the communications "discovery" of the eighties. It can result in valuable insight into accepted community business practices and other artists' experiences with particular businesses, i.e., an art director who was easy to work with or a company that was slow to pay. Pricing standards are easier to formulate when you know the area's going rate. Networking can also lead to jobs and possible co-oping of skills: You might be able to supply to a client some style or service that another artist can't. The other artist might recommend you for the job outright or the two of you could combine your skills to meet the client's needs. If it's an outright recommendation, return the favor when an appropriate assignment arises.

Offer to give free lectures or to teach classes. The local Boy Scout troop might not sound like the place to drum up business, but Boy Scouts have parents, and enthusiastic endorsements from their youngsters stick in their minds. Local colleges, universities, and high schools offer night classes. As the new PR director for a local organization is taking your class to learn a graphic-arts skill that will make her newsletters more pow-

erful, you can be offering to do a brochure for her at a reduced rate in exchange for a credit line. Even if no concrete jobs arise, you certainly gain a reputation as the local graphic arts "expert." The publicity you receive in the school's class brochure doesn't hurt either.

FREE PROMOTIONAL OPPORTUNITIES ABOUND

Cincinnati graphic artist Christine Cotting teaches a class at the University of Cincinnati and puts out a special-interest flyer for the continuing education department. It lists her class and several others; of course, her class gets top billing. The university pays for the printing and postage and does the mailing. She creates the mailing list and gets a free promotional opportunity. She also designed the nameplate for the department's periodical newsletter and did the job gratis with the stipulation that she receive a credit line. The department also did a front-page feature in the premiere issue on her class and her work. It was all free exposure that elicited response.

Chris also donates finished artwork and design services to WCET, Cincinnati's PBS television station, to be auctioned off during its annual fund-raising event. She not only gets great publicity and the chance to see her work and name on quality television, but she also meets potential buyers by volunteering her time to work at the auction. She's received a job offer from a business owner and fellow volunteer while posting auction bids and has gotten names of contacts out of the blue by having her name recognized when working the phones.

Join organizations. For example,

the chamber of commerce and the Rotary Club increase business contacts; if you're female, also investigate the local businesswomen's support groups that compile business directories and recommend each other to their business contacts. Look in the Yellow Pages for other area business organizations that can be of use to you.

Most art organizations cater to fine-art interests; if there is a local graphic-arts organization, join it immediately. (If not, think about starting one; someone has to take that brave first step.) Also investigate the national graphic-arts groups, such as the Graphic Artists Guild, the Artists Equity Association, and the National Cartoonists Society, which are concerned with professional standards, artists' rights, and fair business practices. You might not be able to speak in person on these issues, but by joining such an organization, you're lending your financial support to others' efforts on your behalf.

Membership in interest-related organizations promotes your professional image and helps you keep abreast of what's occurring in your field. See the abbreviated listing in the Resources section following this chapter. For a more extensive compilation, check the *Encyclopedia of Associations*, which lists names, addresses, and functions of associations nationwide. It's indexed by subject and geographic location to help you in your search for the associations right for you and is available in library reference sections. (See the list of directories in the Resources section following this chapter.)

ADVERTISING IN CREATIVE SERVICES BOOKS

Creative services books, also called

trade books, are volumes published with graphic artists' and designers' names and addresses and examples of their work. Illustrators and designers pay to advertise in them, with the costs ranging from several hundred to several thousand dollars depending on the scope of the book and the size and type of ad. Generally, the cost to the artist is less in regional books than national ones, less for black-and-white reproduction than color. The books are distributed to or purchased by art and creative directors who want access to a variety of illustrators and designers.

Some of the national creative services books are *Adweek Portfolio*, *American Showcase*, the *Creative Black Book*, and *Madison Avenue Handbook*. Regional books include the *L.A. Workbook*, *RSVP*, and the *Chicago Creative Directory*. Some are specific to illustrators; others to designers. (Check the Resources section for publishers and addresses.)

Because it's impossible to predict accurately the financial potential of assignments received from advertising in one of these books, think hard before you invest a large sum. The first assignment from a $5,000 color listing could pay back your investment; or the listing could produce not a single call.

Here are some points to help you make your decision:

You should be well established in your profession before spending this much money on marketing/self-promotion. You might spend on one listing as much as you would on your normal marketing activities for an entire year. Be certain your budget justifies it.

You must have absolutely outstanding samples to include in your ad. You'll be one of many top graphic artists competing for a buyer's attention.

Know the audience for the book(s) you're considering. Contact the publishing firm to find out who uses the directory.

Some of these books cover only one city and its surrounding area; if you're outside the region, your chances of seeing a cash return from the ad are greatly reduced. There are too many local artists for the book's users to bother calling you. Even some of the national books focus primarily on major metropolitan cities, so be sure your location is working *for* you before you place an ad.

Compare rates. A few of the large urban areas support more than one book and these publications may be competitive in pricing.

Check on the additional services the publisher offers. Some supply the artist with free reprints of an ad; others charge. Some give access to mailing lists for your interest; others will do a promotional mailing for you. Some give no additional services.

Find out how the books are distributed to potential buyers. Some publishers distribute books free; others require purchase. If the book must be bought, ask the publishing firm how many were sold during the previous year.

Buy or borrow the book(s) you're most interested in. Call some of the graphic artists who advertised and learn what results their ads brought.

APPROACHING THE CLIENT

Potential clients are approached in two ways: in person and through the mail.

The In-Person Interview

Everyone gets nervous going to interviews, but interviewing gets easier the more you do it. The better pre-pared you are, the more comfortable you're going to be. Your challenge is to arrive at each interview prepared to meet the needs of this potential client.

The art buyer is a person with a budget, a time schedule, a deadline, and 60 million other things on her mind. What does she want from you? She wants briefly to meet you and to see terrific artwork presented clearly so she can quickly determine what you do and how well you do it. If she thinks that what she sees meets her current or potential needs, she'll explore further into your experience to judge how well you meet deadlines and conduct business. Lastly, she wants something on hand to remind her of your work and to tell her how to reach you when an assignment comes up. Your portfolio and printed marketing tools meet every one of these requirements.

Some basic business protocol must be followed when setting up interviews:

Always make an appointment. Do not think for a minute, no matter how large or small the potential client, that the art buyer is going to stop everything to see you because you "happened to be in the area and thought you'd drop by." It can happen, yes, but it's unlikely. In the business world, everyone lives on a schedule, and an appointment is your way of grabbing a piece of someone's business day. You want the prospect's full attention on your work and if he's expecting you there is reason to hope that he's carved out time *only* for you.

When you call to make an appointment, speak slowly and distinctly, immediately giving your name and reason for calling. Be friendly and courteous to the person answering the

Javier Romero believes in putting all he can afford into top-quality advertising because the work generated has justified his investments. This $5\frac{1}{2}'' \times 10\frac{1}{2}''$ four-color mailer printed on coated cardstock was designed for and ran as an ad in the the *Creative Black Book*. Although his characteristic circular signage at lower left duplicates the name/phone information at the top, its importance is in the consistency of its use on all of his marketing and promotional pieces. The man-with-suitcase logo is the other image he uses repeatedly. This mailer promotes Romero's work with samples, a menu of services, a corporate and agency client roster, and a testamentary list of awards.

phone; many times he or she knows more about the inner workings of the company than its president and can be a wellspring of information and an ally when you don't seem to be making the right contact. If you don't know the name of the art-services buyer, ask who is in charge of reviewing artwork for free-lance assignments, who handles advertising, or who produces the newsletter or annual report. Write that name down on the 3″ by 5″ index cards used to record all calls, and ask for an appointment.

Some firms, frequently those that receive a high volume of requests from artists for portfolio reviews, set hours one day a week (or every two weeks or once a month, depending on their needs) when the person in charge of buying artwork reviews portfolios. If this is the case, the person answering the phone should tell you these hours. Some reviewers allot a specific amount of time for each artist—ten or fifteen minutes—and schedule only the number of reviews a given block of time will accommodate. If this is the case, ask to have your name added to the list for a specific day. Others simply take artists on a first-come, first-served basis and when the time is up, the unreviewed artists go home to try again at the next opportunity. These reviews, especially the ones with no scheduling, can be frustrating. They tend to be impersonal and, if you're near the end of the line, you can be the victim of reviewer "burn-out"—the buyer gives your portfolio only the most superficial run-through because he's looked at so many. *But,* if the reviewer sees in your work that certain something he's been looking for and offers you an assignment or at least schedules a longer review, the time and frustration probably have been worthwhile. You have to decide for yourself if you'll attend this type of review; there is a definite time and energy investment; on the other hand, this is the only way you'll have your work seen by some firms.

If you set up an appointment several days ahead of time, call the day before to confirm it. Schedules go topsy-turvy even in the most organized situations; and the call can save you a needless trip. The art buyer might have to postpone and reschedule, but better that than a rushed review with her mind on other, more pressing issues. If, for some reason, *you* can't make the appointment, phone as far in advance as possible and reschedule it.

Dress for the interview according to the business standards of your community. You are there to conduct business, and that's the image to convey. Flamboyant or garish dress might be acceptable at art school, but in the business world it smacks of unreliability and can even be an embarrassment to the art buyer if she wants to introduce you to one of *her* clients or business partners. Arrive a few minutes before the scheduled hour and compose yourself. Don't rummage through your materials or review your planned remarks; preparation should have been done before you left the studio. Sit and relax; get comfortable with the environment.

No one can predict exactly how each interview will be conducted, because no two situations are exactly alike. But if you treat each person with respect, believe in your art, maintain confidence in your business abilities, remember that you have rights and prepared well, you'll come out a winner regardless of whether or not you get an assignment.

When you actually meet the art buyer, offer a firm handshake and direct eye contact. Even if you're cringing on the inside, look as if you possess self-confidence and, most important, confidence in your work and your ability to meet the buyer's art needs. When you believe your work is good, that belief is expressed without words in everything you do.

Have all your materials at your fingertips even if this requires a small briefcase or small bag in addition to your portfolio. Don't walk in weighed down with large, awkward cases or numerous cardboard rolls containing original posters. You'll appear both overwhelming and disorganized.

Your portfolio should fit comfortably in the space available on the reviewer's desk (one reason your portfolio preferably should not be larger than 20" by 30"). The potential buyer should be able to review your work without another word from you. If you have an information sheet point out its location in your portfolio or hand it to him as he begins. If he's interested enough to go through your portfolio to the end (if your work is absolutely inappropriate, he probably won't bother), the reviewer should find your resume placed there (either loose or in a protective sheet) so that he can immediately move to reviewing your background and experience.

Questions are bound to be asked. Some art buyers ask first, then look; other ask while they're looking; still others wait until they're all finished reviewing your work. Keep your mouth closed and let your artwork do the talking until the reviewer asks a question. Take your cue from him; don't distract him with superfluous comments just because you're nervous. Use this "empty" time to look around the office—what kind of flyers, business cards, brochures are on the bulletin board? If none, with what has he surrounded himself? What kind of an impression is he giving you: terrifically organized or wildly frantic? This can be important information when it comes time to un-

derstand an assignment or have business dealings with him. It may also be helpful in planning a followup mailing to supply something to be posted where it can be seen frequently.

If your portfolio is in slides, you'll have less opportunity merely to sit and observe. It's good to find out ahead of time if your potential client has viewing facilities, but the smart graphic artist always takes a small handheld viewer to appointments "just in case." Hand viewers are not expensive; many are battery operated and provide a back light and a small magnifying screen. You don't want your appointment to go down the tubes because the reviewer's projector bulb burned out that morning; a viewer gives you an alternative to a light table or the light from a window or desk lamp.

The physical arrangement of the office may dictate how much of a role you play in the slide viewing, but generally speaking stay in the background physically. Usually you'll be able to give a verbal description during the viewing; if the art buyer doesn't want this, have your information sheet available. Some reviewers will place your slides on a light table and quickly scan them, selecting only a few to view blown up. This is disappointing when you've gone to the trouble of organizing them and when people like me are telling you the importance of sequence, but there's not much you can do about it. Be thankful she was interested enough to pull some of them out. It's most frustrating when reviewers use only the light table with no magnification because you know much of the impact and detail of your work isn't being seen.

Once the interview is over (take your cue from the buyer), tell the prospect how much and why you'd like to free-lance for her and present your leave-behind packet. Only when it's quite obvious that there's absolutely no interest in your work should you not present materials for the files. Even then there's reason to leave one or more samples, just in case—art directors have a tremendous attrition rate and what one hates, the next one may like. It never hurts to be on file.

Use interviews as learning situations—analyze each of them to determine what you could have done differently or what materials might have better served you. If you feel you did everything right and still did not get an assignment, then you may simply conclude that your work wasn't what this client needed at this time. Nothing more, nothing less.

Luck and timing play almost as important a part in landing an assignment or making a sale as do talent and good business skills. And, believe it or not, the more you're faced with rejection, the clearer this point becomes: you learn to put rejection into its proper perspective.

If the art director offers an assignment on the spot, don't panic. Some of us are so tuned in to expecting rejection or noncommitment that when an offer arrives we're so stunned we turn to jelly. Most of all, listen carefully to what the art director is saying. If he's outlining a specific project, take notes. Packing a pad and pencil in your case makes this operation smooth. If he's expecting you to quote a price, the important points you should know now are:

- The number of illustrations or designs.
- How the illustrations or designs will be used.

- The intended market (such as an ad for a nationwide campaign, editorial illustration for a children's book, greeting cards or stationery).
- The deadline.
- The reproduction rights he's expecting to buy.
- What he considers "final" art—are you expected to provide color overlays, typesetting, and so on?

Once you have all this information, ask for some time to figure out your time and rates so you can provide a price quote that's fair to both of you. Some artists can simply go into another room for a few minutes and arrive at the figure; others need to go back to the studio and regroup. If you fall into the latter category, tell the client you'll call within the hour with your price quote—and be sure you do. Don't leave him hanging.

Whether or not an assignment arises at the end of the interview, the first thing to do when you return to the studio—after figuring necessary quotes—is fill out the prospect index card with information pertinent to the interview: date, impressions of the experience and the response, type of presentation you made, materials you left behind, type and schedule of follow-up planned, and results of the interview as they become apparent.

DETERMINING AND NEGOTIATING A PRICE

Pricing work projects becomes easier as you gain experience and familiarize yourself with the practices of the marketing field, but even the most experienced artists sometimes underestimate a job. There is no magic formula to make this process mistake-free when you're starting out, but one way you can begin to arrive at a price is to establish for yourself a daily or hourly rate. Thus, if you believe the assignment you're considering will take you three days to complete, multiply your daily rate times three; if it will take only a half a day, divide your daily rate by two. Then factor in these other considerations:

- The scope intended for the work—for example, if it will have national exposure, your base price should be raised.
- The complexity of the assignment—if you feel your base price doesn't adequately reflect the effort that will go into this work because of its complex or intricate nature, raise the price.
- The deadline—if the deadline presented to you is extremely tight (such as overnight), add to your base price; meeting impossible deadlines is a special service.
- Other costs, such as research, typesetting, travel expenses, model fees, and consultation fees should be included in your price, thus raising the base, or be negotiated as expenses billable to the client.
- The rights purchased—the more rights the buyer wants to own, the higher the fee.
- Your reputation and experience as an artist—the more experienced you are, or the greater your reputation, the higher the price.

The *Graphic Artists Guild Handbook: Pricing and Ethical Guidelines* contains price averages for virtually all fields of illustration and design ob-
tained by the guild through a national survey. Use these prices as guidelines only; there may be great differences between the price ranges quoted and what *you* can actually charge. Your price can vary according to where you live, inflation, market conditions, and all of the points mentioned previously in regard to pricing. The handbook is invaluable especially because it explains ethical standards for the graphic-art industry, business and legal practices, and professional issues, such as work-for-hire contracts and artists' moral rights. It also contains standard contract forms and information on business management. If you can't locate a copy at the library, write the Graphic Artists Guild at 30 East 20th Street, New York NY 10003.

If the price you've arrived at or some other term the client has mentioned is not acceptable, remember that negotiation is acceptable and an acquired art. A *mutually* satisfactory agreement is your goal; neither of you should be out to win at all costs. The only way the client is going to know your needs and wants is for *you* to tell her. Work cooperatively and try to put yourself in her place. Speaking slowly and distinctly forces a rushed client to slow down and listen to you. Be willing to compromise, but don't totally capitulate just to get the assignment. Pick an aspect of the assignment where you believe there might be room for negotiation and ask her the reasoning behind her thinking. For example, many art directors routinely ask to buy all reproduction rights to a work—a request that has your higher price tag attached to it. The buyer might not actually *need* all rights; you can point out that if she is willing to purchase only first North American serial rights (appropriate for magazines, newspapers, etc.), your price can be lower. Suggest alternative solutions to problem areas *and* listen to her solutions until you reach an agreement you both can live with comfortably. By negotiating with patience rather than anger or ego, you'll be remembered as an artist who's "flexible" and "easy to work with"—valued qualities in your business.

The Mailed Art Submission

Selling your work through the mail has some definite advantages and disadvantages. First let's look at the advantages.

If you're one of the many extremely shy artists who'd rather give up a finger than try to sell your work in person, mail solicitation can be the answer for you. Since all contact is via the mail or telephone (indeed many regularly selling artists have never met face-to-face with the client they've been dealing with for years), you can let your artwork be the salesperson and not worry about your visible embarassment when discussing money or being rejected.

Mailed submissions allow you to contact numerous potential clients at one time and this means your work can be seen simultaneously by prospective buyers all over the country. Time and money are saved because you can plan a mailing package, have all duplicates and printing done at once and collate all package materials in assembly-line fashion.

Marketing through the mail is especially advantageous for the part-time artist who isn't free to meet with clients during normal business hours. Mailing packages can be put together and sent out in the evenings and over weekends.

You can reach markets that normally wouldn't be available to you for in-person contact if you live away from urban areas, and can do it when *you* have the time, not when the client has time to see you.

There are several disadvantages: You never get to talk about your work in person, to point out why it's right for the client, and why *you* are the artist to do the job.

You don't know for certain that the art buyer is ever really seeing your work or if it's being sidetracked by an assistant or secretary who'll stack it up with others for the boss to see "someday." Unless you use a reply card and the prospect sends it back to you, there's no certainty that it's been filed as you'd like.

It can be costly to put together numerous mailing packages, especially if you're using samples like slides or photographs that you'd like returned. Some recipients return samples; others don't.

There's usually no feedback regarding your submission unless you get an assignment. During an in-person review you can "read" facial expressions or body language and sometimes can ask an art director for a professional opinion of your work or portfolio. With a mailed submission, this opportunity doesn't exist.

Only you can decide if a mailed submission is right for you. Some artists swear by them and others never use them.

If you plan to contact a potential client through the mail, your mailing package is taking over the role you and your work performed at the interview. Thus your highest priority is to make it *communicate*—visually through the design of your enclosures and work samples; verbally through your cover letter and the written text

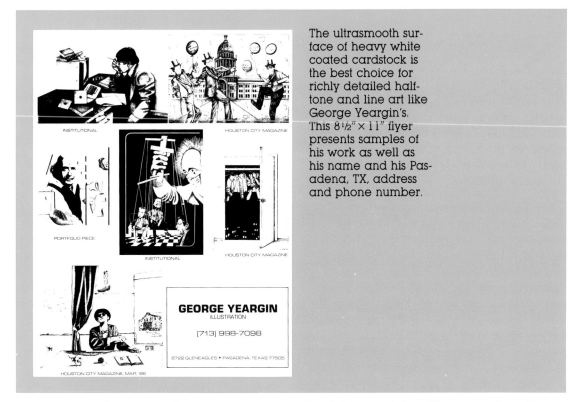

The ultrasmooth surface of heavy white coated cardstock is the best choice for richly detailed halftone and line art like George Yeargin's. This 8½" × 11" flyer presents samples of his work as well as his name and his Pasadena, TX, address and phone number.

on your marketing tools.

Your cover letter is a sales pitch and your chance to explain the who, what, why, where, when, and how of you and your art.

The who and what. Who are you and what do you do? Use clear but descriptive language. Say what you said on your letterhead and business card, but enlarge upon it. Don't just say that you're an artist; tell *what kind* of artist and specifically *what type of art* you do. As with every other tool, gear your descriptions to the client or market area you're approaching.

The why and where. Why are you writing to this client and why would you like to be selected for an assignment? Highlight your strongest personal points as an artist—that you're

flexible, meet deadlines, work well within a budget, take direction easily over the telephone, and so on. If you know of some strong positive aspect of the client's business or product—they make better mousetraps or produce award-winning catalogs—incorporate it to explain why your work is appropriate for the firm or why you would particularly like to free-lance for this company. Everyone responds favorably to praise, and the art buyer is no different.

The where is a brief listing of where you've sold your work before, a minilist of clients who will be of particular interest to your current potential client. If you haven't sold anything yet, list places where your work has been used—jobs that you've done on a volunteer basis for example. If you don't have this credit either, ignore this point.

The when and how. These two can be combined to wind up your letter either by stating when and how you can be contacted for an assignment or when and how you plan a follow-up to your package. You can also mention here what action you'd like the reviewer to take with your package—file it for future reference, return your samples to you in the enclosed SASE, or retain some samples and return the rest.

When you're preparing to write this letter, review your answers to the strengths questions in Chapter 2. This will focus your strengths and put you in a positive frame of mind to promote your work. Also refer to the copywriting guidelines in Chapter 3.

The cover letter should never be longer than one page, typed on your letterhead. Always address your letter and your mailing package to a specific person even if it means a brief long-distance phone call to the company to find the name of the appropriate person. Verify the correct spelling of the art buyer's name and if it's not apparent from the name, find out whether you're contacting a male or a female.

The other materials you enclose should be unified visually and convey as much information about you and your work as possible. Include a brochure or a flyer-mailer-resume combination, both of which accomplish the same informational purpose. A business card is optional but it's best to send one—you have no way of knowing if your contact pins them on a board or keeps those of special interest in a desktop filebox for immediate reference.

The types of samples you send depend on whether your work is in black and white or color and whether you expect their return. If you work

in color or want to show examples of tearsheets without sending the actual pieces, enclose slides or photographs. Photographs can be held together with a clear acetate folded sheet and a plastic slip-on spine. Slides should be in a plastic slide sheet cut to accommodate the number of slides. Or all of your materials can be placed in a folder with pockets. *Just be certain your final product fits an 8½″ by 11″ file drawer.* For more specifics of handling samples, see Chapter 3.

If you don't want your samples returned, three to five are sufficient. If you do want their return, as many as fifteen to twenty can be sent to give the buyer a broader selection. Beyond twenty is overkill. Consider the mailing weight and cost of each package and decide whether you're really giving fresh images with each sample or merely trying to impress the reviewer with quantity.

If you work in black and white, mail less-expensive black-and white photographs, photostats, or photocopies and don't request any return. Slides work well too, but the extra cost and return request make them a choice only if the other sample types don't do justice to your work or if you're sending images of final products that don't reproduce well with these other methods.

Do not send your entire portfolio, original work, or tearsheets (unless you have hundreds to get rid of). The likelihood of their being lost, mislaid, or unreturned is too great to justify the risk. The only possible exception is if you've had previous contact with the prospective client, who has requested specific items from you. And even then, if you're not comfortable with the client's level of integrity don't risk your whole portfolio.

The art buyer will probably not

wish to buy the samples you send; rather these will provide a "feel" for your style, medium, and technique. Keep this in mind when you're planning your mailed samples: view them objectively to see what and how well they communicate about your work.

Your mailing envelope can be one specially designed and printed to match your stationery or a plain envelope purchased at an office supply or stationery store. Self-adhesive labels, printed to match your stationery, customize standard envelopes. Buying them in bulk saves money. For added protection you can invest in "bubble" envelopes (lined with a sheet of plastic filled with air bubbles), envelopes lined with a thin sheet of Styrofoam, or extra-strength envelopes. These cost extra but survive mailing virtually unscathed. Remember to place sufficient postage on the SASE for the weight of the return package.

If you are including a reinforced return envelope, you will probably not be able to fold it. You'll need to buy two envelope sizes, one the correct size for returning the samples, the other large enough to accommodate the full size of the smaller envelope and the mailing package.

As detailed earlier in this chapter, keep a 3″ by 5″ index card on each mailed submission containing all pertinent information, the date mailed, and any response received.

If you're using the U.S. Postal Service for your mailings, a free booklet, *A Consumer's Directory of Postal Services and Products*, is available at your local post office or by writing Consumer Advocate, U.S. Postal Service, Washington DC 20260-6320. This booklet provides information on the mail services offered by the U.S. Postal Service, proper addressing and

packaging, special services such as insurance, claims, special delivery and certified mail, military mail and international mail, mail fraud and mail problems, postage meters, passport applications, and self-service postal centers. Armed with this knowledge, you can select the services most appropriate to your mailing needs, whether business or personal, and know what to do if a problem arises.

When addressing your mailing package, address only one side of the envelope, be sure your return address is in the upper-left corner, and don't decorate it with cutesy stamps or dire handwritten warnings. Writing "First Class" or "Do Not Fold" once is sufficient; better yet, ask the postal attendant to stamp it when you mail it or buy your own stamp. Be sure to include the addressee's zip code; the post office suggests that for the most efficient processing you capitalize everything in the address, eliminate all punctuation and use the two-letter state abbreviations.

First Class is the fastest mail class for your mailing package if it weighs twelve ounces or less; if it isn't letter-size, be sure it's marked First Class or use a green-bordered large envelope.

Priority Mail is First Class mail that weighs more than 12 ounces and less than 70 pounds. It receives the same two- to three-day service as First Class. Priority Mail stickers are available free from your local post office.

Second Class mailing is available only to publishers and registered news agents who have the authorized privilege of mailing at second-class pound rates.

Third Class mail is often referrred to as bulk business mail, but it can be used by anyone since there are two rate structures: one for a single piece and one for bulk mail. Your parcel must weigh less than sixteen ounces. Frequently the difference in postal costs between Priority Mail and Third Class is only a matter of a nickel or dime, and it's worth the faster service to go with Priority Mail. If you're doing a large mailing, however, consider Third Class because the nickels and dimes add up. Contact your local post office for further information on the regulations governing a bulk mailing.

Fourth Class (Parcel Post) is for packages weighing one pound up to seventy pounds but is the slowest of the postal services. Unless the price difference is exorbitant, consider using Priority Mail instead.

It's tempting to think you need more postal service than you really do when you're mailing out packages that can mean so much to your career. Some artists feel that more attention will be paid to their package if it's sent special delivery, registered mail or Express Mail. Probably not. Consider these if you're mailing final art after an assignment, but not for your sample package; you're spending money needlessly.

There are some items you can request from the post office that will be helpful to you: Always ask for a cash receipt for your recordkeeping and as proof of purchase to the IRS should you be audited.

Certified mail, available only for First Class pieces, provides you with a mailing receipt and a record of delivery maintained at the recipient's post office. For an additional fee you can request a return receipt which provides you with proof of delivery.

United Parcel Service (UPS) accepts packages up to fifty pounds and, besides its regular service, offers a two-day air service and a next-day service

in some areas. Numerous overnight air-freight services also abound, but these aren't really necessary for sample packages. Check into UPS services if you'll be mailing large packages or into the overnight services for deadline items when you're mailing final art after an assignment. All are willing to give rate and restriction information over the phone or have available brochures outlining their services.

There are a number of overnight air express services to get your package to a client in hours. They are costly and only to be used when an assignment deadline demands it.

Drop-offs

Some art directors don't want to spend the time for an interview but do want to see your portfolio. They'll request that you "drop-off" your portfolio and leave it for their review. Normally the drop-off is on one particular day or morning, but some will accept them anytime. A specific time is usually set for pickup as well. If you're not informed of a pickup time, ask how you'll be notified or when you should return.

Are drop-offs a good idea? On the plus side is that at least your portfolio is seen, and it's one more opportunity for an assignment.

On the debit side, there's no guarantee your whole portfolio won't be lost or damaged, and feedback is minimal. Further, you're the one doing all the work—making the trip to drop it off and the trip back to pick it up.

Whether to use drop-offs is a personal decision. Try it once or twice if the situation arises, and see how you feel about it.

UPDATING YOUR MARKETING STRATEGY

Depending on the scope and frequency of your marketing endeavors, after six months it's time to take stock of where you are and where you're heading. Some surprising changes may have occurred that require re-evaluating your tools and target market(s):

- You find yourself doing work you hadn't anticipated when you began, as one client has recommended you to another you hadn't thought to approach.
- The field you first contacted isn't supplying you with enough assignments to support you.
- You're finding success locally, but most of your marketing efforts are nationwide.
- You simply need some fresh images in your marketing materials and portfolio.

Careers evolve, and what was right for you six months to a year ago may not be right for you today. Set aside a day (yes, *mark it on your calendar*) to review your portfolio, marketing tools, and index cards. Think hard about your current situation—list what you like about it and what you don't. What can change the negatives? A different field, better market research, better pricing standards, schooling to increase skills, more thorough understanding of business concepts, membership in a graphic artists' organization?

In a review of your marketing tools, ask yourself the following questions:

- Does your resume need updating so current clients are listed?
- Does the artwork on your brochure look outdated?
- Does the written text reflect your current professional image?

- Would you enjoy a new look to your stationery and business card?
- Have you moved or changed your phone number?

Go through your index file and delete cards over a year old from which you've had no response. Enough money's been spent on them. Review the ones left—do they spark any new ideas? Seeing your successes and failures in black and white clarifies why you've been successful with some clients and not others.

This is also the time to ask yourself how you feel about free-lancing as a whole. Do you still feel mentally, physically and emotionally good about it? If not, is it time to evaluate and update your overall life-style? Depending on your current circumstances, should you consider free-lancing only part-time while bringing in a steady income from another source, or vice versa—drop full-time employment and devote more time to free-lancing?

When you've decided what you need to freshen your marketing approach and professional outlook, go back to square one and proceed just as you did when you first began. Establish short- and long-range goals. Your short-range goals might once again include printers' price quotes and reproduction of your work. Your long-range goal might be to set up appointments with buyers in an untried marketing field with short-range goals of new market research and mailing-list preparation supporting the long-range goal.

Consistent re-evaluations keep your career fresh and growing. The form your marketing takes may change with time and experience, but marketing never stops. To be a successful graphic artist you must rely on marketing to let consumers know what your product or service is, that it's available, and where and how to buy it. Otherwise you won't be successful—no one knows who you are.

THE CHANGING GRAPHIC ART SCENE

As with any business, the graphic art scene is evolving and growing. Computers have entered the artist's life, not to replace you but to give you the means of creating a different type of art more quickly. Electronic media are opening doors to creativity undreamed of twenty years ago.

As the business changes, your marketing and promotional efforts can change with them. Don't be afraid to open your eyes to untested areas for advertising yourself. Explore the possibilities and costs of renting a billboard, running ads in newspapers and general-circulation magazines, starting your own newsletter for businesses, buying airtime on radio or a Yellow Pages ad, placing an ad on a local cable TV station or a listing on a computer bulletin board. Just because these outlets aren't frequently used by graphic artists doesn't mean they can't be. You might have to be the first—but you'll be remembered. Today's business competition sometimes means we have to risk standing out from all the rest, not only in our talent but also in letting clients know it exists. Use your imagination in your marketing and promotional efforts as you do in your artwork, and see how far it takes you.

CHAPTER FIVE CHECKLISTS

The In-person Interview

Follow these steps for a successful in-person interview:
- [ ] Make appointment with the art director or art services buyer
- [ ] Confirm appointment day before
- [ ] Dress according to prevailing business standards
- [ ] Arrive few minutes early
- [ ] Be totally prepared with materials
- [ ] Pack materials in excess of portfolio in briefcase or small bag
- [ ] Meet art director with firm handshake and direct eye contact
- [ ] Appear confident in self and work
- [ ] Have portfolio organized for easy review
- [ ] Have information sheet available during review, if applicable
- [ ] Answer questions only; don't interrupt review with comments
- [ ] Have resume available for review
- [ ] Present leave-behind at interview's end
- [ ] Complete contact index card once home
- [ ] Plan follow-up mailing to art director

The Mailed Art Submission

To maximize your mailed art submission:
- [ ] Plan contact with numerous clients at one time
- [ ] Organize to fit standard file size
- [ ] Include a cover letter, art samples and printed marketing/promotional materials
- [ ] Include SASE if materials to be returned
- [ ] Complete contact index card on each mailed submission
- [ ] Plan follow-up mailing

Pricing Considerations

When setting your fee for an assignment, consider:
- [ ] Scope of use for final artwork: national scope = higher fee
- [ ] Complexity of assignment: more complex = higher fee
- [ ] Deadline: short deadline = higher fee
- [ ] Additional costs to you to complete assignment: either billable expenses or added to fee
- [ ] Reproduction rights purchased: more rights = higher fee
- [ ] Artist's reputation and experience: the greater these are, the higher the fee

Updating Your Marketing Strategy

It's helpful to regroup periodically and review your marketing endeavors:
- [ ] Analyze types of clients and assignments you're attracting
- [ ] List successes and failures and analyze list
- [ ] Revise resume to include current clients, interests, awards
- [ ] Review texts on promotional materials for accuracy
- [ ] Change address and phone number if different
- [ ] Review artwork on promotional materials and in portfolio for outdated pieces
- [ ] Evaluate that all materials communicate who you are today
- [ ] Redesign logo, if necessary
- [ ] Dispose of old marketing materials
- [ ] Delete index cards of year-old clients who've not responded
- [ ] Review your budget
- [ ] Evaluate feelings about free-lancing

RESOURCES

DIRECTORIES

Adweek Agency Directory
Adweek Books
49 E. 21st Street
New York NY 10010

Artist's Market
Writer's Digest Books
1507 Dana Avenue
Cincinnati OH 45207

Billboard International Buyer's Guide
Billboard Publications
1515 Broadway
New York NY 10036

The Design Directory
Wefler & Associates, Inc.
Box 1591
Evanston IL 60204

Encyclopedia of Associations
Gale Research Co.
Book Tower
Detroit MI 48226

The IMS Directory of Publications
IMS Press
426 Pennsylvania Ave.
Fort Washington PA 19034

Literary Market Place
R.R. Bowker Co.
205 E. 42nd Street
New York NY 10017

Music Industry Directory
Marquis Professional Publications
200 E. Ohio Street
Chicago IL 60611

O'Dwyer's Directory of Public Relations Firms
J.R. O'Dwyer Company, Inc.
271 Madison Avenue
New York NY 10016

Songwriter's Market
Writer's Digest Books
1507 Dana Avenue
Cincinnati OH 45207

Standard Directory of Advertising Agencies
National Register Publishing Co.
3004 Glenview Road
Wilmette IL 60091

Standard Periodical Directory
Oxbridge Communications Inc.
150 Fifth Avenue
New York NY 10011

Thomas Register of American Manufacturers
Thomas Publishing Co.
1 Penn Plaza
New York NY 10017

Writer's Market
Writer's Digest Books
1507 Dana Avenue
Cincinnati OH 45207

PERIODICALS

Advertising Age
740 Rush Street
Chicago IL 60611

Adweek
A/S/M Communications Inc.
49 E. 21st Street
New York NY 10010

The Artist's Magazine
F&W Publications
1507 Dana Avenue
Cincinnati OH 45207

Billboard
Billboard Publications Inc.
1515 Broadway
New York NY 10036

Business Week
McGraw-Hill Publishing Co., Inc.
1221 Avenue of the Americas
New York NY 10020

Communication Arts
Coyne & Blanchard, Inc.
410 Sherman Avenue
P.O. Box 10300
Palo Alto CA 94303

Compute!
ABC Publications
1330 Avenue of the Americas
New York NY 10019

Dancemagazine
33 W. 60th Street
New York NY 10036

Editor & Publisher
The Editor & Publisher Company, Inc.
575 Lexington Avenue
New York NY 10022

Chicago/Midwest Flash
Alexander Communications, Inc.
212 W. Superior, Suite 400
Chicago IL 60610

Forbes
60 Fifth Avenue
New York NY 10011

Fortune
Time, Inc.
1271 Avenue of the Americas
Rockefeller Center
New York NY 10020

Greetings Magazine
MacKay Publishing Company
309 Fifth Avenue
New York NY 10016

How: Ideas & Techniques in Graphic Design
355 Lexington Avenue
New York NY 10017

Modern Photography
ABC Leisure Magazines
825 Seventh Avenue
New York NY 10019

Popular Photography
CBS Magazines
3460 Wilshire Boulevard
Los Angeles CA 90016

Print
355 Lexington Avenue
New York NY 10017

Publishers Weekly
R.R. Bowker
205 E. 42nd Street
New York NY 10017

Step-by-Step Graphics
Dynamic Graphics, Inc.
PO Box 11192
Milwaukee WI 53215

Theatre Communications
355 Lexington Avenue
New York NY 10017

CREATIVE SERVICES BOOKS

Adweek Portfolio
Adweek Books
49 E. 21st Street
New York NY 10010

American Showcase
American Showcase, Inc.
724 Fifth Avenue
New York NY 10017

Chicago Creative Directory
333 North Michigan Avenue
Chicago IL 60603

Creative Black Book
401 Park Avenue South
New York NY 10016

LA Workbook
940 North Highland Avenue
Los Angeles CA 90038

Madison Avenue Handbook
Peter Glenn Publications Inc.
17 E. 48th Street
New York NY 10017

RSVP
AMSCO School Publications
315 Hudson Street
New York NY 10013

ORGANIZATIONS

Art Directors Club
488 Madison Avenue
New York NY 10022

Artists Equity Association
PO Box 28068
Central Station
Washington DC 20038

Cartoonists Guild
30 E. 20th Street
New York NY 10003

Center for Arts Information
1285 Avenue of the Americas
New York NY 10019

Graphic Artists Guild
30 E. 20th Street
New York NY 10003

National Cartoonists Society
9 Ebony Court
Brooklyn NY 11229

Society of Illustrators
128 E. 63rd Street
New York NY 10021

INDEX

Accomplishments list, 58, 59
Adams, Norman, 20-21, 39, 78, 99
Advertising agencies, 1, 6, 19, 20, 25, 26, 27, 51, 56, 89, 91; description, 5, 83; resource directories, 84, 85, 86-87; trade publications, 87
Art product analysis, 21-24
Art publishers and distributors: description, 3
Art/design studios, 1, 6, 19, 25, 48, 56; description, 5, 83; resource directory, 84-85
Artist's Market, 14, 86-87
Associations, 14, 25, 107; description, 4; resource directories, 85, 86, 101
Audiovisual firms; resource directory, 86, 87

Billboard International Buyer's Guide, 86
Biographical sheet, 61
Book publishers/ing, 19, 25, 26, 88, 98; description, 3, 83; resource directories, 85, 86, 87; trade publication, 87
Brochure, 1, 5, 6, 38, 48, 62, 73, 74, 77, 90, 91, 95, 96, 98, 99, 105, 110, 113; description, 52-53
Business card, 14, 26, 61, 74, 78, 90, 91, 95, 97, 98, 105, 110, 113; description, 55
Businesses, 24, 25, 26, 114; description, 5-6; resource directories, 85, 86; trade publications, 87

Client, 5, 9, 19, 56, 57, 58, 59, 64, 65, 68, 89, 90, 91, 96, 97,.107; how to locate, 21, 83-88
Client contact, 37; mail, 2-6, 14, 25, 26, 73, 87 88, 89,

90, 97-98, 108-112; in-person, 2-6, 25, 26, 87, 88, 89, 90, 95-97, 102-106; social, 26, 99
Client list, 84, 87, 88, 95, 99, 109
Clip art firms; description, 3
Cold call, 19, 20
Communication Arts, 16
Computer, personal, 13, 14, 15, 96, 97, 114
Consumer's Directory of Postal Services and Products, 111
Contact sheet, 41, 42
Copyright notice, 41, 44, 45
Copywriting, 3, 22, 30, 52, 53, 64, 77-78, 95, 110, 113
Cotting, Christine, 100
Cover letter, 14, 53, 90, 91, 97, 98, 108, 109, 110
Creative services books, 101-102
Crolick, Sue, 27-30, 33

Deadline, 19, 25, 27, 79, 95, 102, 106, 107, 109
Design Directory, The, 84-85
Diamond, Doug, 48
Drop-off, 19, 46, 112

Encyclopedia of Associations, 86, 101
Envelope, 14, 65, 68, 111; description, 53-55

Finances, 2, 9, 16, 27, 30, 33, 37, 38, 51, 64, 73, 88, 89, 90, 91, 96, 99, 101, 109, 113
Flyer, 20, 25, 73, 74, 78, 90, 91, 95, 96, 99, 105, 110; description, 62, 64

Goals, 2, 9, 37, 95, 113
Graphic art, 24, 25, 38, 46, 52; beliefs/attitudes about, 8-9, 113; as a business, 1-2, 26; definition, 1; mar-

ket fields/areas, 2-6; as a product, 1, 7, 27; publications, 16; samples, 37-47
Graphic Artists Guild Handbook: Pricing and Ethical Guidelines, 107
Graphic design, 3, 5, 24, 25, 28, 29, 30, 37, 38, 48, 52, 53, 95, 108; portfolio, 47, 48; samples, 47-48
Greeting card publishers/ing, 1, 2, 19, 20, 25, 26; description, 3, 83; resource directories, 85, 87; trade publication, 87

How: Ideas & Techniques in Graphic Design, 16
IMS Directory of Publications, The, 85, 86
Index cards, 87, 96, 97, 98, 104, 106, 111, 113; master card, 97
Information sheet, 41, 44, 45, 46, 47, 90, 91, 105; description, 68, 70
In-person interview, 47, 52, 62, 88, 89, 90, 95-97, 102-106, 108
Institutions, 25; description, 4
Invoices, 53, 91; description, 74-75

Johnson, Nancy, 30, 64, 75

Kay, Patie, 6, 55, 84, 98

Labeling, 41, 42, 43, 45, 46
Labels, 47, 91, 97, 111; description, 75, 77
Leave-behind, 43, 45, 51, 64, 65, 88, 91, 106; description, 70, 73-74
Lecturing, 26, 100
Letterhead, 28, 29, 61, 70, 90, 91; description, 53-55
Literary Market Place, 85
Logo, 5, 6, 27, 29, 37, 42, 52, 53, 55, 64, 75, 77, 91

Magazines, 1, 5, 19, 20, 25, 26, 56, 89, 91, 97, 114; description, 2-3, 83; resource directories, 85, 87; trade publication, 87
Mailer, 21, 27, 78, 90, 91, 96, 110; description, 64-65
Mailing list, 14, 87-88, 99
Mailing package, 20, 38, 39, 41, 42, 43, 44, 45, 46, 47, 52, 54, 62, 64, 65, 90, 91, 97, 98, 108-112
Mailings, 26, 48, 97-98; follow-up reminder, 64, 65, 90, 91, 96, 97, 105, 106, 110; self-promotional, 99
Market research, 8, 19, 24, 51, 58, 83-88, 91, 99, 113
Marketing calendar, 90, 95, 96, 97, 98, 113
Marketing fields/areas, 21, 37, 51, 52, 56, 65, 91, 99, 109, 113; definition, 20; descriptions, 2-6; how to locate, 24-26
Marketing package, 37, 42, 52, 61, 77, 89
Marketing plan/strategy, 19, 20, 21, 22, 27, 29, 30, 90, 95, 98, 99, 112-114
Marketing tools, 19, 95, 113; art samples, 37-48; definition, 20; development of, 88-91; printed, 51-59, 61-62, 64-65, 68, 70, 73-75, 77; as self-promotion, 78-79
Mental health, 8, 10-11, 113
Music Industry Directory, 86

Negotiation, 106, 107, 108
Networking, 26, 78, 87, 110
Newsletter publishers/ing, 4, 6, 99; description, 4; resource directory, 87
Newspaper publishers/ing, 5, 6, 20, 25, 26, 114; description, 4, 83; resource directories, 85, 86, 87; trade publication, 87

O'Dwyer's Directory of Public Relations Firms, 84
Office equipment, 13
Organization membership, 26, 99, 100-101
Original artwork, 37, 38, 45, 51, 88, 89, 91, 110; description, 45-46
Orlin, Richard, 14-15
Over the transom, 20

Performing arts groups, 25; description, 4; resource directory, 86; trade publication, 87
Photocopier, personal, 13, 14, 15
Photocopies, 37, 88, 89, 110; description, 45
Photographs, 37, 47, 48, 88, 89, 91, 108, 110; description, 41-43
Photography, 39, 47, 95; equipment, 49; exposure "bracketing," 50; film, 49; hiring photographer, 48-49; photographing own works, 49-50; self-promotional, 52, 64, 78
Photography lab, 40, 42
Photostats, 37, 88, 89, 91, 110; description, 43-44
Portfolio, 7, 20, 38, 41, 42, 43, 44, 45, 46, 47, 48, 84, 88, 90, 91, 95, 102, 104, 105, 108, 110, 112, 113; development, 51
Portfolio case, 46, 51
Postal classifications, 111-112
Presentation, 47, 51, 70, 91, 106; definition, 20
Pricing, 106-108
Print, 16
Professionalism; attitude, 11-12, 21; business environment, 12; with clients, 12; dress, 12, 104; image, 52, 90-91, 113
Public relations firms, 6, 19, 25, 91; definition, 20; description, 5, 83; resource directories, 84, 87

Record companies, 25, 91; description, 4, 83; resource directories, 86, 87; trade publication, 87
Record keeping, 2, 13, 16, 99, 112
Reference number, 41, 44, 45, 46, 47, 68
Rejection, 6-9, 106
Reply card, 97, 98, 108; description, 65

Reproduction rights, 106, 107
Resource directories, 84-87
Resume, 14, 21, 46, 53, 74, 90, 91, 105, 110, 113; chronological, 55-58; description, 55-59, 61-62; functional, 58

Samples, 19, 51, 73, 74, 78, 84, 88, 89, 90, 91, 95, 96, 97, 98, 101, 106, 108, 110, 111; duplicates, 40, 89, 90, 108; graphic art, 37-47; graphic design, 47-48; original artwork, 45-47; reproductions, 37-45
SASE, 65, 68, 110, 111; definition, 20
Schedules, 20, 99, 100, 102, 104; interview, 95; mailing, 97; work, 11, 12, 13, 95
School work, 51
Self-mailer, 52, 53, 64, 91
Self-promotion, 1, 16, 26, 37, 64, 78-79, 89, 91, 95, 99-101
Simultaneous submissions, 20
Slide sheets, 41, 110
Slides/transparencies, 37, 47, 48, 88, 91, 105, 108, 110; description, 38-41
Songwriter's Market, 86
Standard Directory of Advertising Agencies, 84
Standard Periodical Index, 87
Step-by-Step Graphics, 16
Studio, independent, 11-16
Success, 9-11
Syndicates; description, 4-5

Target market, 20, 22, 83
Taxes/Internal Revenue Service, 13, 16, 112
Teaching, 100
Tearsheets, 38, 46, 88, 89, 91, 110; description, 46-47
Thomas Register of American Manufacturers, 85

Vinyl cover/sheet, 42, 44, 45, 47, 48
Volunteerism, 26, 99
Writer's Digest, 14
Writer's Market, 85-86